First Steps in Ballet

First Steps

in Ballet

Brian Shaw

With special photography by Jesse Davis

octopus

Contents

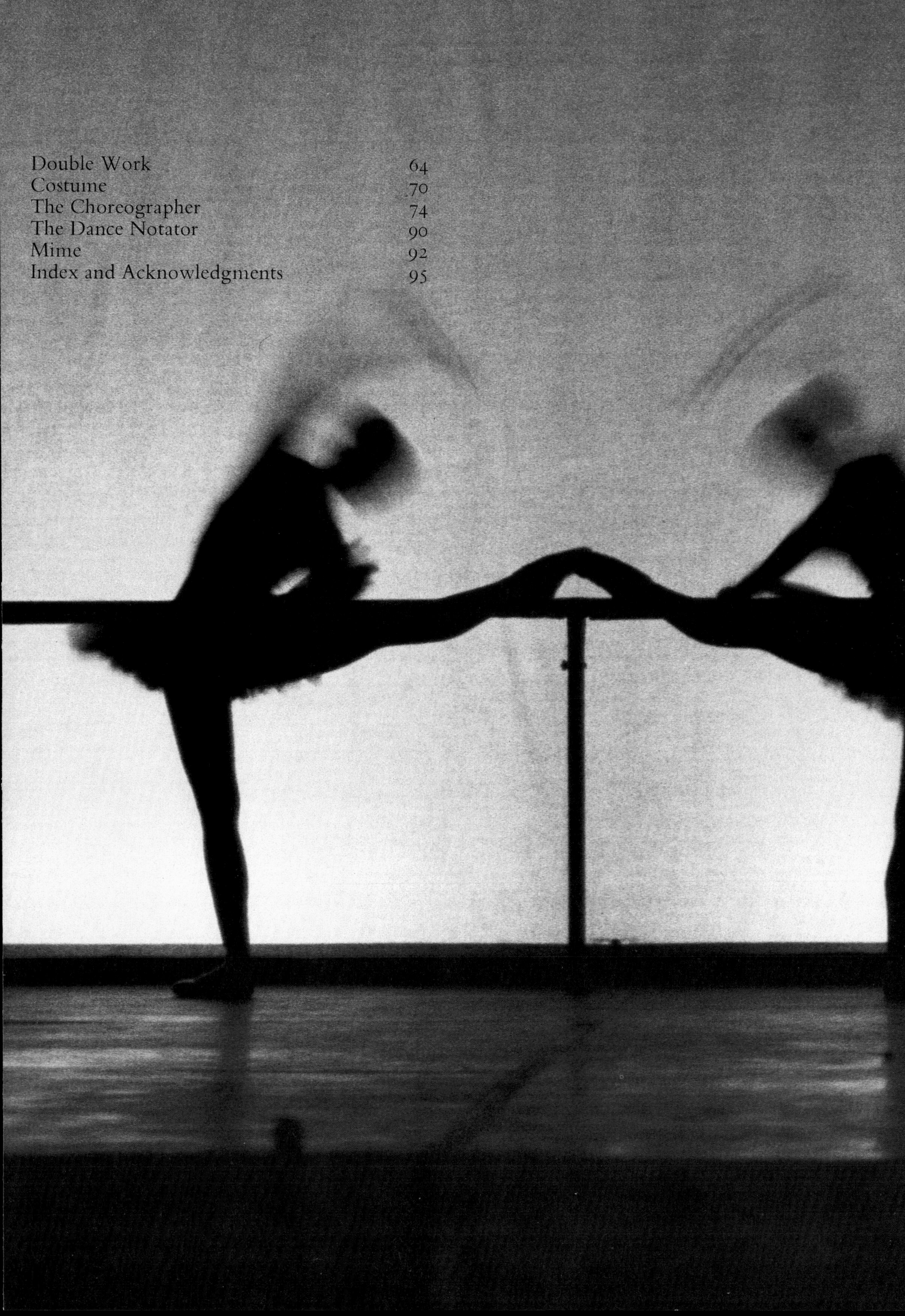

Foreword

It gives me particular pleasure to introduce this guide to the world of ballet as I have worked closely with Brian Shaw as dancer, teacher and producer of my ballets, such as *Les Patineurs*, in Europe, Canada and America.

The importance of sound training from the earliest years cannot be overemphasized as it is during this time that the dancer acquires the important basis for future development. A simple error, repeated many times in class, can become a major problem in the years ahead and can ruin the chance of a rewarding career in ballet.

As Principal Teacher of the Royal Ballet Brian Shaw works closely with some of the great dancers of our time and in this book he shows the work which has gone into making them into fine dancers and artists and how a young dancer can work towards the same end.

This is a clear picture of the hard work a ballet student must do in order to combine musicality with strength; perform a spectacular step with apparent ease and realize the visions of the choreographer.

Frederick Ashton

Sir Frederick Ashton, CH, KBE, OM

Brian Shaw wishes to express his sincere appreciation for all the help given to him by Craig Dodd in the preparation of this book.

Introduction

Ballet technique has developed over the centuries from formal dances at court, which were little more than very elegant walking, to the peak of brilliance we see on the stage today.

Although the very first steps were taken in Italy the real establishment of ballet as you might recognize it took place in France. An official school was established at the Paris Opera and ballet masters began organizing the steps into a syllabus much the same as the one you might be studying today.

From that time French has been used to describe the various positions, steps and movements of the ballet and you could expect to hear the same instructions in a ballet class in Auckland that you would hear in Zagreb. It is the universal language of ballet, just as Latin was the universal language of the Roman Church. Usually you will find that a simple translation tells you what sort of step to expect, for instance *ballion* suggests bounce and *rouetté* means to whip, but I will explain them as we go through the class.

Just as there are different national schools and styles of teaching, such as the Russian, the French or the Danish, so you will probably be following a course in one style and working for the examinations of that syllabus. I am not going to follow a particular syllabus here so you might notice little differences from the way you are taught. This does not mean your teacher is wrong! I must emphasize that this book is not meant to replace dancing classes. I have tried to take a course between all these different schools which should give you a good idea of ballet technique in general. Where there are very clear variations, such as in the positions of the arms, I will point them out. If I don't, and you spot them, I suggest that you just listen to your teacher and don't try to argue with her!

In writing this book for you and arranging the photographs one thing has become very clear. You can't learn to dance from pictures. However carefully they are taken and presented it is not possible to show you such important things as the rhythm for an exercise, the phrasing of a sequence of steps in the centre or to teach you musicality. Neither big, fast-moving turns and jumps nor small beats of the feet can be shown precisely. These are all things for which you must depend on your own teacher.

What I *can* do is to warn you about common faults, explain that little bit more about individual steps and also try to give you some good reasons why you do certain steps in certain ways day after day. Every little step has a firm place in the whole plan and if you know a little about that place the whole picture may become clearer to you. I have also used photographs of particular steps in performance to help build up this picture.

I also hope to give you some idea of the world of ballet beyond the classroom; the way dancers and choreographers work, as well as how ballets are written down. I have also included an explanation of mime, so important in one of my own favourite roles, the Widow Simone in *La Fille Mal Gardée*, as well as photographs of some of the world's top dancers in performance.

Two young dancers from the Royal Ballet, Ashley Page and Angela Cox, show you in the photographs the steps and positions as they do them in class every day. They will give you a clear idea of how two working dancers start their day before rehearsal and performance. Of course they will be showing you not only the basic positions and exercises that you will already be doing at the barre, but also the more difficult turns and jumps which you are working towards. This will give you a complete picture of the work which is necessary for the beautiful ballerina to float across the stage or for her Prince to do a perfectly finished jump without sign of strain or the slightest stumble.

After short explanations of terms which you will come across throughout the class we will start with the exercises at the barre, gradually preparing your body for the exciting big steps; the turns, the jumps in the centre. And then on to the stories of some favourite ballets which you may, one day, dance in if you are lucky enough and work hard enough to join a ballet company.

Left: Brian Shaw in Sir Frederick Ashton's *Enigma Variations* which brings to life the friends of the composer, Edward Elgar.

The Basic Positions

The feet

The five positions are the basic positions of the feet from which you will always start or end a step or series of steps. They are all turned out, which means that your feet are in a straight line from toe to heel and heel to toe.

These positions were not invented by one person at a particular time, but grew from the steps of court dance when it was thought that a delicately pointed foot looked attractive. Gradually the turned out position, which starts at the hips and not just at the ankles, became necessary to give the dancer freedom of movement for the more demanding steps. We first find them written about in France in the seventeenth century when the ballet master, Beauchamp, put the practice of the time into some order, but it was not until the next century when full turn-out, that you would recognize today, became common. Then Carlo Blasis, the great Italian teacher, wrote down the beginnings of the sort of training you are now working at.

Before that time dancers had long recognized the importance of beautiful line but did not have the necessary technique to achieve it. Some even used artifical aids to keep them in a turned-out position!

When you think about it, it is easy to see why the turn-out is necessary. Imagine a dance in which the legs could only swing forwards and backwards and you can see how limited it would be compared to the ability you have, through turn-out, to describe a great arc in the air from front to back.

First Position
Your legs are together and your heels should be touching. The feet form a straight line. As you stand in this position you must also be conscious of your posture before we move to the next position. Your weight should be evenly balanced and you should think tall and stand straight with your head high. Your body should feel as though it is lifting from the hips, which will encourage a nice slim waist, and there should be no

1: First position with the appropriate *port de bras*. Always try to work with your heels together.

2: Second position with the feet about one and a half lengths of your own foot apart. Your weight will be evenly balanced.

3: Third position with *port de bras*.

4: Fourth position crossed. Your foot will be opposite the first position for which the turn out must be good.

5: Fifth position with the arms *en haut*. Your feet should be firmly crossed and your arms in a natural curve. No bent elbows or fingers.

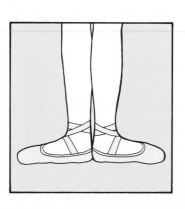

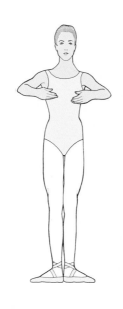

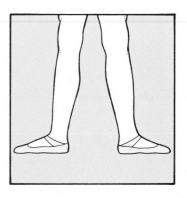

sense of strain. Breathing should be even and deep from your diaphragm. You are going to use up a lot of extra oxygen during these exercises.

Second Position

Your feet should be apart by about one and a half lengths of your foot and the weight of your body should shift to balance evenly.

Third Position

Your fully turned-out feet are partly crossed so that the heel of one foot fits into the hollow of the instep of the back foot. You will not see this position very often during performances, but it is very important to you as a way of working towards the much more difficult, but very necessary fifth position.

Fourth Position

You will learn two versions of fourth position in the same way that you will master third position before fifth position. The open fourth position will come first. In correct sequence you will do it after third position, but it looks like a first position with one foot about 12 inches in front of the other. Crossed fourth position looks like fifth position with one foot in front of the other. Naturally you will progress to this just as you progress towards fifth position itself. You see a variation of this position used as a strong start to big turning movements.

Fifth Position

This is the most difficult position to achieve, but after you have mastered a good third position you will see how fifth position is a natural progression from it. The heel of one foot is against the toe of the back foot, maintaining the full turn-out.

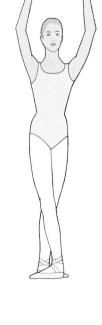

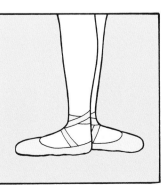

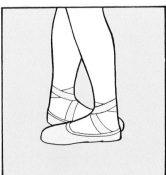

The arms, head and eyes

The carriage of the arms is called the *port de bras*. Graceful arms are as important to you as turn-out. A beautiful pose can be spoilt by the broken line of an arm or a hand which shows strain. Your arm should always be in a natural curve without being angular and your hand should always be relaxed with the middle finger suggesting the natural extension of the line of the arm. Never point!

The positions of the arms complement the set positions of the feet and you will usually find the two positions used together. However the positions of the arms are not so carefully defined and there are variations of each position according to the different syllabuses.

First Position
Your arms should be lightly curved downwards with the fingers held a few inches apart making a natural rounded shape from the shoulders.

Second Position
Your arms should be held out to the side in a natural line from the shoulders. The curve should be soft and not angular with a feeling of continuing length rather than stretching out. Take care that your elbows do not droop and make an ugly line.

Third Position
You keep one arm in second while the other arm is maintained in first position.

Fourth Position
One arm remains in second while the other arm is raised in a natural curve high above the head with the hand held softly.

Fifth Position
Both arms are raised above the head with the elbows curved slightly, but not sufficient to break the natural curve of the arms to hands which should be a few inches apart.

The *port de bras* such as fifth position can be performed with the arms high as described (*en haut* or *couronne*) held out in front of the body (*en avant*) or as described for first position (*en bas*).

Work at developing good *port de bras* as the arms are vital in creating a beautiful line.

The carriage of the shoulders, neck and head is called *épaulement*. Noble bearing is important to all dancers and the correct placing of the head in relation to the *port de bras* is vital in maintaining a harmonious picture. The eyes too must reflect that harmony.

When the basic positions of the feet are performed with the feet flat on the ground they are called *à terre*. Second and fourth positions can also be performed with the tip of the toe touching the floor with the heel raised and are referred to as *pointe tendue*.

For the girl the same positions apply when on point and for both boy and girl they can be performed on half-point, known as *demi-pointe*.

Below: Note how the smooth line of the arm continues right up through the hand to the little finger.

Left: The feet showing *demi-pointe* (half point) which will be used during many exercises, such as *petits battements*.

Right: Cou de pied back

Far Right: Cou de pied front

Retiré front, toe just under the knee

Passé with the toe at the side of the knee, higher than *retiré*.

The Barre

All classwork starts at the barre. The exercises warm up the body and prepare the muscles for the more spectacular, and so more demanding, work in the centre. It is still wise to do some warming up by yourself in readiness for the barre, because if you are not properly warm you can sprain your joints, or strain muscles or injure yourself in some other way. Professional dancers work out their own warming exercises, although they do sometimes take short cuts and wear plastic pants and colourful woollen leg-warmers. Definitely not advisable for you no matter how theatrical it looks!

It is very important to remind you that the photographs in this book show you each exercise from one side only. You will know from your own experience that every exercise must be done from both sides to make your training perfectly balanced. Each leg takes its turn to be either the working or the supporting leg; although you must realize that the 'supporting' leg is really working too. Each exercise is also repeated several times and will be done starting from each of the different positions of the feet. The correct *port de bras* will also be used as every exercise must be complete even though at first sight we may only appear to be exercising one foot.

As I have already said I cannot show you exactly the rhythm of each step but I will try to convey the feel of the movement in each case; the crispness of the *frappés* or the smoothness of the *fondus*.

The work at the barre is designed as a gradual build-up towards the centre exercises. After the warming *pliés* we work from the feet up to the hips with exercises designed to strengthen the leg muscles. We slowly increase the amount of work and time they can sustain remembering that at the barre it is the length and nature of the exercise which builds up stamina, not the degree of difficulty. The repetition of each exercise imprints the steps and positions into both muscle and brain.

We start work at the barre with the *pliés*. Hold the barre lightly as a support (as shown below). Do not grasp it tightly as this will not only produce strain, but also stop you developing natural balance.

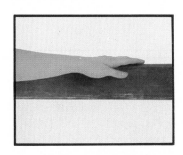

Far Right: Etudes. The opening section of this ballet consists of exercises at the barre.

Right: Angela's hand rests lightly on the barre.

14

Pliés

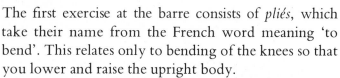

Ashley and Angela ready at the barre to start the *pliés*. Angela will do them in first position and Ashley in second.

Slowly down through the *demi-plié* holding the back firm and the hips square.

The first exercise at the barre consists of *pliés*, which take their name from the French word meaning 'to bend'. This relates only to bending of the knees so that you lower and raise the upright body.

The *pliés* prepare the legs for the work to come as well as increasing mobility and turn-out. By the time you do two *pliés* in each position you will be feeling the warmth of the increased circulation.

You start with your legs straight and then go into a knees bend, keeping your back straight, your hips level and your hand lightly resting on the barre for support. You should keep your shoulders lined up above your hips and your knees over your feet with the weight of the body evenly balanced between your two feet. Your body should be well pulled up and your waist firm and you should remember not to stick your bottom out—a natural thing to do and a bad mistake to make as you will see if you look at yourself in the studio mirror.

When you first learn *pliés* you will do them in the first, second and third positions only, later adding both open and closed fourth and fifth (replacing third) to your repertoire.

As you move down and then up the movement should be smooth and even, like pressing against a large spring.

You will keep your heels firmly on the floor except when you do the *pliés* in the 'closed' positions (first, third and fifth) when they should be allowed to rise naturally.

The point at which you feel it right for them to begin to rise is usually taken as the position of *demi-plié* which can be a position on its own account.

You will see it used as the start of *pirouettes* and both beginning and ending of jumps, giving them the soft landing so necessary.

Lack of *demi-plié* can lead to over-muscled legs and can spoil the finish of jumps.

It is possible to *plié* on one leg, but this really becomes a further exercise, *fondus*, which we will deal with later (*see page 25*).

Both dancers have reached the *full plié* position. Notice that Angela's heels have raised naturally, while Ashley's are firmly on the floor.

Rise through the *demi-plié* with your *port de bras* changing in harmony.

The *demi-plié* position, this time with Angela in fourth position crossed and Ashley in fifth position.

Full *plié* is reached before you return through *demi-plié*.

Tendus

Your starting position for the *tendu* will be a good closed fifth.

Your leg and pointed foot move forward to a *tendu devant* . . .

The exercise done to the side starting from second position. . .

. . . and returning to fifth position back . . .

. . . and then back to fifth position.

. . . and then on to *tendu* back, before closing again to fifth position.

The *tendu* is the stretching of the leg and foot from a closed position to an open position and back, taking the weight of the body onto your supporting leg. Your leg should be well turned out from the thigh down, with your foot well stretched. Your toe does not leave the floor.

Tendus should make you foot conscious. You should be well turned out from the thigh down, with with the toes well-stretched, too. Never be tempted to curl the toes as though grasping the floor for balance during any exercise. The centre of balance should always be kept by the body and the legs, leaving the foot free to become perfectly arched and stretched.

The *tendu* can be done to the front, the side and the back. You will start in fifth position, sliding your foot out till the toe is just touching the floor and then smoothly back. You should remember to keep a nice straight posture during this exercise as well as doing the correct *port de bras*.

Just as with the *glisseés* which follow, this exercise will help develop swift footwork for the fast *allegro* exercises to come later.

Glissées

You will start from a good fifth position front . . .

and then move smoothly to *tendu devant* . . .

Glissé to the side will start from a good fifth position and move to *tendu* in second before sweeping . . .

. . . up to the *glissé* position just two inches from the floor before returning through the *tendu* to fifth position once again.

. . . and through to the *glissé* when your toe will be raised from the ground . . .

. . . before returning back through the *tendu* to the starting position.

A *glissé* back starting from a good fifth position will move cleanly through the *tendu* back with the torso held erect. Do not lean forward.

Glissé means to glide and this is just what the foot and leg do during the exercise. It is the same type of movement as the *tendu*, but the toe this time leaves the floor by about two inches. The toe is last to leave the floor and first to return, thus ensuring that the foot is beautifully pointed and a nice instep displayed.

As with the *tendu* you should feel a pressure through the floor on the way to the pointed and raised foot and again on the way back, and the exercise can again be done to the front, the side and the back.

Rond de Jambe à Terre

David Wall and Lynn Seymour in a scene from Kenneth MacMillan's production of *Romeo and Juliet*.

During this exercise, which means circling the leg on the ground, your toe will draw a semi-circle on the floor. Your leg and foot will be fully stretched. You should feel the movement coming from your hip and have a very definite sensation of the movement in the hip-socket. This will show you how the exercise is helping develop your turn out. With good erect carriage, you can start from first or fifth position.

Starting from a *tendu* behind your leg will draw the semi-circle cleanly and smoothly through the side and then the front positions before returning to close back in first position

If you were to include the preparation, which every exercise will of course have, the sequence of moves will be; from first or fifth position to *tendu* in second with a *demi-plié*, then to *tendu* back. You will start from flat feet, stretch the toes during the drawing of the semi-circle, but remembering that they never leave the ground before returning to the flat position.

As your work progresses you will be able to do this exercise with the foot raised off the ground, but do not confuse this with the later *ronds de jambe en l'air* during which the raised thigh is held firmly and only the lower leg moves.

Already you will be feeling your body working more smoothly and with this gradual progression your muscles will be warm and you may perspire. But do not strain for effects. Remember the importance of working with even effort.

A good fifth position to start before taking the foot out . . .

. . . to a *tendu* front, the leg then drawing a semi-circle to the side . . .

. . . shown here from a different angle at the barre before closing back to fifth position.

Battement Frappés

Frapper means 'to strike' and that describes exactly the feeling of these beats. They are hard, sharp movements where the ball of the working foot brushes the floor lightly as though it were red hot!

This exercise will be performed on half or three-quarter point and you will see that the foot is flexed in the *cou de pied*, not pointed as we have shown earlier.

Start at *cou de pied*, foot flexed, then sharp to a stretched foot out in second position at the side and back just as sharp. The movement is coming from your knee which must stay at the same height during the exercise and should not lift which it might feel like doing as the foot returns smartly to the flexed *cou de pied*.

You can perform this exercise to the front and to the back. The action must still retain the snapping quality if the exercise is going to develop flexible ankles and precise foot movements that are required of a dancer.

In this photograph Ashley is shown in the starting position and Angela the half-way position. The foot then returns to the original position.

From a *cou de pied* position the leg slowly unfolds to . . .

. . . an *attitude* front with a *demi-plié* before straightening the supporting leg . . .

. . . as the working leg unfolds fully to the front. All the time, the back must be kept firm, the hips square and the joints working smoothly.

Left: A scene from *Etudes*, Harold Lander's ballet, originally choreographed for the Royal Danish Ballet in 1948.

This is one exercise where the name very easily suggests the quality of the movement. We have all eaten fondant chocolates and think of their creamy melting consistency! As you lift your working leg, while bending the supporting leg in a *plié*, it should feel as though it is pushing its way smoothly through a pile of fondant cream!

This slow, smooth working is both warming the legs up for the exercises to come, as well as raising the leg that little bit more in preparation for the *grands battements*. Then it will be required to swing as high as it can. At the same time the supporting leg is, for the first time, carrying the weight of the whole body while bending into a *plié*. This is going to be useful for the beginnings of jumps, as well as the soft landings you will want to make.

You will start the exercise with a *tendu* to the side. The supporting leg does a small *plié* while the working leg is brought to *cou de pied devant*. It then works smoothly through to *attitude* in front, developing to a full stretched leg raised forward. At this point the extended leg is straight and turned out and the toe is pointed.

The movement is elastic as though at each point the foot and leg were working against a great spring which is slowly unfurling the leg, whether the exercise is being done to front, side or back and through the same returning sequence ending up in the starting position.

Ronds de Jambe en l'Air

During this exercise, in which your leg describes a circle in the air, you will realize that we are reaching a stage when the working leg is expected to do much more and that all the muscles are being worked harder.

To be exact the leg must draw an oval, not a circle, with the smoothness that must go into stirring a Christmas pudding. Your working leg is raised from the ground, through a *tendu* to second position. It then draws the oval reaching a *retiré* position with the big toe at the side of the knee. Your hips must be kept level, with the thigh held high while the lower leg is working. Your upper body must be held straight and should not move, except of course to maintain a good *port de bras*.

As with all the exercises it must be balanced, so not only will you do it from both sides, but you will also draw the oval in an outwards direction which is called *en dehors*, as well as in an inward direction, known as *en dedans*.

You will see variations of this exercise used *en l'air* particularly in the great Danish ballets such as *La Sylphide* or *Napoli*.

Top to bottom: Starting from a fifth position, the leg is raised to second position through a *tendu* at the side. The knee rotates so that the foot draws an oval in the air. The centre picture shows the innermost point of the oval before returning back to a full second position before reaching the ground through a *tendu* back to fifth position.

Opposite: Marcia Haydée and Richard Cragun, two of the stars of the Stuttgart Ballet, in the *pas de deux* from *Romeo and Juliet*, created by John Cranko who founded the company.

Retiré

Retiré position to the front with the toe just under the knee.

Retiré means withdrawn, and so when applied to a ballet position it refers to bringing the well-stretched foot up until the toe is just under the straight supporting knee, with the knee of the raised leg well turned out to the side. A *passé* position is similar, but the stretched toe of the raised foot is at the side of the knee. *Retiré* can of course also be done to the back of the knee.

When performing a *retiré*, the foot should go to *passé* fast like a jack-in-the-box. Next time you see *Swan Lake*, look out for Odette, the Swan Queen, performing these simple steps in her solo in the last part (the *coda*) of the *pas de deux* of the second act.

Développés

This is once more an exercise where the name tells you the sort of movement to expect. In an unfolding, developing, series of movements your working leg, with the foot well pointed, will be slowly lifted through a *retiré* position to an *attitude* and ultimately to a fully extended *arabesque*.

It is important that this exercise is done slowly and evenly. Although your body is now fully warmed up you are lifting and stretching your limbs to their fullest point, at the same time pulling up the abdominal muscles. Carriage and balance are also vital as you will soon be doing *attitudes* and *arabesques* during the *adage*, or slow exercises, in the centre work.

Développés should be done to the front, back and side to ensure not only balanced development, but also a beautiful line through the body. At its fullest point your *développé* should have a feeling of continuity out beyond your body into the audience.

Top: Développé to the side which will literally have developed to this high position through *passé*. The body must be held erect and not allowed to bend to one side to counterbalance the rising leg.

Left: Développé back to an *arabesque* which will have been reached through *retiré* position, slowly unfolding through to an attitude. To achieve this height the body must move forward, forming a natural balance with the raised leg.

Petits Battements

These 'little beats' are short, sharp beating movements of the feet done to prepare you for the fast-moving beaten steps of the centre work.

Starting from a *cou de pied* to the front and with the foot flexed, the foot then beats rapidly behind as though kicking away a football from behind the supporting leg, before returning to its starting position in front.

The tempo of this exercise can vary, but the object is always to achieve swiftness of movement as your working foot wraps from the front to the back of your supporting leg; swiftness which will be especially important in steps such as the *entrechat* later.

The work is done by your lower leg, from the knee, with your thigh held steady. As usual it will be well turned out, too.

Right: A scene from John Cranko's *The Taming of the Shrew* which is full of amusing characters and brilliant humour.

Below: In this photograph Angela shows the position to the front and Ashley has his foot behind. If you imagine these positions alternating rapidly while staying close together you will have a good idea of the way the beat is taking place.

Grands Battements

Both Angela and Ashley are doing a *grand battement* to the front. It is at its highest point, having moved through the *tendu* and the *glissé* on the way up. It will pass through these same positions on the way down to starting position.

Big Beats. And that is just what they are. Just as the *petits battements* concentrated on the work from the knee controlling the fast movement of the feet, so the *grands battements* concentrate on the work of the whole leg from the hip socket.

Grands battements* are the controlled throwing up of the leg to its maximum height without letting your hips swivel or slip out of alignment. They will increase your extension and prepare you for the fast *allegro* work, just as the *developpés* prepared you for the slow *adage*.

You will notice that I say 'controlled' throwing up of the leg, as you must remember the intermediate positions. The leg goes up through *tendu* to *glissé* and up,

before returning in the reverse sequence. You may pass through these stages fast, but you must remember that they are there, even though you go quickly up. You may be more conscious of them on the slower, controlled return to the floor. Leave the floor as though it is red hot; return as though you think it still is!

When you perform the *grands battements* to the front and side you will keep a straight, balanced posture. When you perform them to the back your body will move forward a little to allow the leg to achieve a good height, but you must not do so exaggeratedly. Your body must still maintain a good line, as this backwards movement if maintained would, at its height, of course be an *arabesque*.

Grands battements to the back showing how the body is allowed to tilt naturally forward.

Grands battements to the side in which you can see the natural higher extension which girls usually possess.

Limbering

Above: Stretching the muscles of the upper leg at the end of the barre. You can see how the *port de bras* is maintained even here.

Above right: A back stretch during which you should feel the muscles being further developed.

Right: A sideways stretch during which, though it is aimed at muscles and tendons, the foot is still kept beautifully pointed.

Opposite: Natalia Makarova and Ivan Nagy in the American Ballet Theater production of *Coppelia*.

Now that we have reached the end of the barre section of the class you can do further stretching exercises using the barre as your support. These will stretch the tendons and muscles further, all working towards loosening the body more as well as helping your legs achieve greater height for your *arabesque*.

These are still controlled exercises and it is essential to remember the way you hold your hips, the angle of your head and the use of the *port de bras*.

Not only are you helping the body move easier with these exercises, but by lengthening muscles you can also be slowly changing the shape and appearance of them, something which could prove very important in a stage career.

When the limbering exercises are complete we are ready to move to the centre where the work becomes more complicated and starts to look more like what you see at a performance.

Centre Work

Now that your body is fully stretched and your muscles have been warmed up we move on to work in the centre of the studio. No longer will you have the support of the *barre* as you will soon know if you have been relying on it too much for balance. You will understand why it is important not to grip it too firmly when you come to perform some of those same steps without its help.

The work in the centre is the part of the class which will start to shape exercises into dance. Apart from extending parts of your technique, as I will explain later, it is the first part of your training which will make you aware of the importance of dances as a whole. It is really what dancing is all about.

Technique aside, you will now have a chance to think more about your movements as a whole, to co-ordinate them in a smooth rhythmical way and to develop musicality. Groups of steps linked into *ènchâinments* must be treated as little dances and not mechanically. You will be able to develop your interpretive ability and learn how to use different *tempi* for effect and

how to introduce light and shade into your dancing. You will be aware of your body in the air and how to use space as well as the floor, to give you the accent for steps.

The opening slow section, the *adage*, will develop balance and coordination and introduce *ports de bras* for both arms for the first time now that you are free of the *barre*. You will be learning how to move your body in all directions as well as coping with problems of weight transference.

You will then move on to the turning movements, the small jumps and then the big exciting jumps. Girls will develop their *pointe* work, boys their special strong jumps. Together you will practice the technique of double work; the supported turns, the difficult lifts as well as the exciting tricks which you see in the great classic *pas de deux*.

Act II of *Swan Lake* set at the lakeside.

Positions of the Body

Croisé devant en l'air

Croisé derrière en l'air

Ecarte devant en l'air

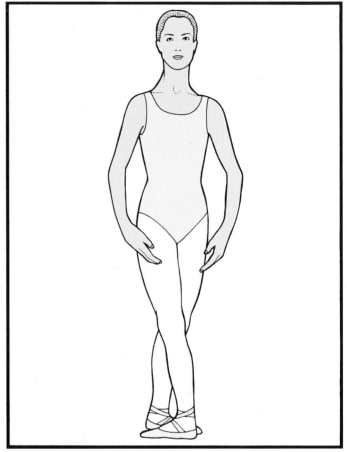

Fifth position *en face*

All the exercises we have done at the *barre* and will do in the centre have been shown either from the side or directly from the front for clarity. They can however all be performed in various other positions all named in relation to how they would be seen by an audience from the front of a stage. Performances would be limited if every step was done straight at the audience or in profile!

The concepts which have evolved have many variations, the most basic being *croisé*, *effacé* and *ecarté*. The working leg crosses the line of the supporting leg in a *croisé* position, but is open in the *effacé* position. The difference is shown most clearly in the drawings below. Although they show positions with both feet on the ground, the same applies when one leg is raised.

In the *ecarté* position the body is again obliquely towards the audience with the working leg opened to the second position, either on the ground or in the air.

All of these positions allow the dancer to appear diagonally in relation to the audience when on the stage and so introduce colour and variety into the basic positions which would otherwise look dull.

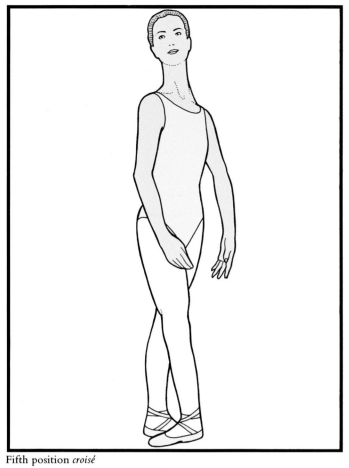

Fifth position *croisé*

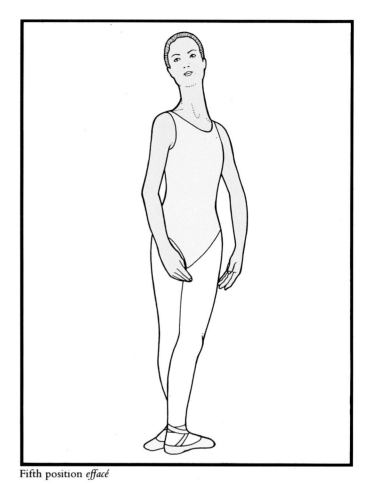

Fifth position *effacé*

Croisé devant, pointe tendu à terre showing 'crossed' appearance.

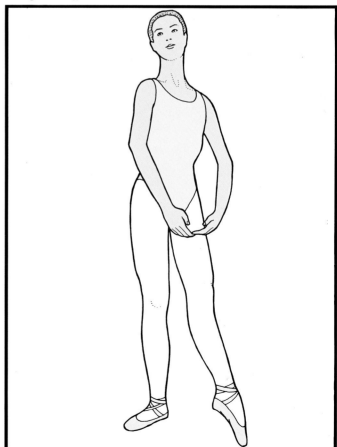

Effacé devant, pointe tendu à terre showing 'open' appearance.

Attitude

The position known as *attitude croisée* was inspired by the famous statue of Mercury by Giovanni da Bologna and was one of the earliest poses to be carefully defined by the famous teacher Carlo Blasis who lived and worked in the first half of the nineteenth century.

It is a pose of great simplicity and like the *arabesque* demands a harmony of position through the arms as well as through the raised leg. In fact one famous teacher Johansson who studied under the great Danish teacher Bournonville and went on to teach himself in St Petersburg, is quoted as saying that it is not enough to do an *attitude*. The dancer must become one!

The pose consists of standing on one leg with the working leg lifted behind the body and bent at the knee. Although there are differences in different schools of teaching you can say that generally the knee should be higher than the foot, although even this convention is becoming outdated. In the West it is usual to have the knee bent almost to right angles, but the Russian school prefers that the angle be not so sharp which makes for a longer line. The knee in any case should be kept well behind the body.

The *port de bras* can vary but it is usual to raise the same arm as the leg with the other arm held in second position (out to the side). It is very important that your hips are kept square and to keep your raised thigh as near to parallel with the floor as you can. This takes strength and balance so you should not strain, but work at it slowly and consistently.

This position will be used for *pirouettes* or the *promenades* and balances of the *Rose Adagio* or indeed in jumps.

Right: An unsupported balance *en attitude.*

Far Right: The radiant Lesley Collier of the Royal Ballet during the Rose Adage in Act I of *The Sleeping Beauty* when Aurora celebrates her sixteenth birthday.

40

Arabesques

The *arabesque* is one of the most basic poses in the ballet. You make an *arabesque* by standing on one leg with your working leg lifted behind the body as high as possible, fully stretched. You will keep the same body position when you raise the leg so that there will be a natural line through the body from the tip of your finger to your toe.

Each *arabesque* has corresponding arms as you can see from the photographs. The carriage of your arms is particularly important and they should feel as though resting on a cloud, with the middle finger of the arm raised in front in a line with your nose.

As you are lifting the leg back, directly behind the fifth position and *not* behind the second position, you will feel that your body will naturally want to tilt forward from your pelvis. It is finding the correct amount of tilt, which in any case should never be excessive, to give your best line which is the art of the arabesque. You will see some dancers who do not lift their leg very high and it may appear rather straight, but because the line is natural and there is a harmony throughout the body it can look as beautiful as a very high extension.

Arabesque penchée is the exception to the rule about tilting the body. This is the pose you may have seen in the opening of the ballet *La Bayadère* when a long line of ballerinas enter, each doing an *arabesque penchée*.

Your body, and this is a step girls will perform mostly, is allowed to tilt forward so that the foot of the leg raised behind is higher than the head. Although appearing to lean forward you must not allow your pelvis to tilt too much as it is really the leg pushing up which forces the body forward and not the back falling forward. The arms, too, will have been lowered with the torso, but the line must be kept and the wrist must not drop.

Right top: À la seconde shows the extension of the leg that should be aimed for in arabesque.

Right centre: First arabesque

Right: Second arabesque

Opposite above left: Third arabesque

Opposite right: Arabesque penchée

Opposite below: The Kingdom of the Shades scene from La Bayadere which is always danced to perfection by the corps de ballet of the Royal Ballet.

Pirouettes

The word *pirouette* refers to a group of turning steps, for both boys and girls, in which you move on one leg while the other is held in a particular position. This position will give you the name of the particular type of turn. It may be *en attitude*, *en arabesque* or *à la seconde* for example, but I will start with some general points you must watch and then the most basic *pirouette*.

You will learn to perform a *pirouette* in both directions. *En dehors* is the direction away from the supporting leg, turning outwards. *En dedans* is turning towards the supporting leg, turning inwards.

Depending on the starting position, which I will explain later, your weight will in general be on the leg which is going to support you, and you will learn to turn on *demi-point*. You will see dancers rise higher than this (and, of course, girls will do their *pirouettes* on pointe as well), but you will find *demi-pointe* best for doing more than one turn.

In the *pirouettes* the use of the head is very important. You must find a 'spot' which means focussing your eyes on some point directly in front of you, and as you begin to turn you will look at this to the last moment, looking for it again as you complete the turn. In other words the head is last to leave and first to return. This will stop you from feeling giddy and losing balance.

The simplest, most basic, *pirouette* will consist of one complete turn starting from second, fourth or fifth position. Each of these starting positions has a particular use. You will start to learn from fifth, although as you progress you will find that this has limitations. However, to begin you will gradually work up to a full turn, through a quarter turn, then half and then a three-quarter turn.

In fifth position you will be able to find the centre of balance of your body more easily before you do a *demi-plié* which will give you the push-off to turn. Then you raise your working leg to a *sur le cou de pied* position, rise on to *demi-pointe* and turn. You will move smoothly through the *demi-plié* and not hold that position as the turn should be one continuous movement.

Once you have mastered the basic turn you will move to the second and fourth starting positions. Although boys and girls will learn both, in general boys will use the second position, and girls the fourth, much more.

Fourth position gives a more powerful push off which will mean a greater number of turns is possible, although you must be careful not to throw yourself off balance. You will see turns done in this way in Aurora's solo in the first act of *The Sleeping Beauty*.

Starting from fifth position make a good *demi-plié* with heels firmly on the ground . . .

It is also one of the starting positions boys will use when performing a *pirouette à la seconde* particularly when turning *en dedans*. Second position will be used when turning *en dehors*.

In either case the turn is the same, having the working leg raised in second position with the foot well pointed and the leg in a line with the hip.

The position of the arms can vary, but generally they should be in the second position or *en haut*. Whichever position is used the arms must hold it naturally and be neither rigid nor used to throw the body round.

You will see many dancers, nearly always boys, performing *pirouettes à la seconde*. A rare use of this step

. . . *relevé* and up to *retiré* starting to turn immediately . . .

. . . and once around returning back to closed fifth position with arms in *demi-bras*.

for the ballerina is in the *Don Quixote* pas de deux.

Pirouettes en attitude, as with *pirouettes en arabesque* are advanced steps which will not be attempted until late in your training, or when your teacher decides you are ready for them. Both can be performed in either direction. *En attitude* will start from fourth position back for boys and will often end not back in the starting position, but with the raised leg extended to an *arabesque* when the body has stopped turning.

Pirouettes en arabesque which you will see used beautifully in *Les Sylphides* and *Swan Lake*, must be beautifully controlled and performed slowly. Performed in a series, with a *relevé* in between each turn, as in *Les*

Patineurs, they are a fiendishly difficult part of the ballerinas repertoire and require much practise and perseverence.

Everything in ballet has to be worked for and practised, but the *pirouette* and the general ability to turn is something which can be a natural talent. This does not mean that you must not work at it if you have been blessed with this talent, but if you feel the movement well do not try to force it too much.

If you are not a natural, do not force turns either. Two controlled turns, smoothly executed, are much more effective (and beautiful) than multiple spins and hit-or-miss endings.

Petit Allegro

We move now to a part of the class which consists of small jumps specially designed as a preparation to warm the legs up for the bigger jumps to follow. All these jumps are done from two legs and you will always land on two legs, with your weight evenly balanced so that neither foot is taking too much strain.

All these jumps should go through the foot from heel to heel to build up grace and control. You press into the ground to push off up into the air. The toe is last to leave the ground, which of course means that your instep is well stretched.

Soubresauté is literally a quick jump starting from fifth, through a *demi-plié* then up into the air. Stretch your feet as you go up and then return to the ground with another soft *demi-plié* back into fifth position. While up in the air only the front foot will be visible to someone looking directly at you from the front if you are keeping a good fifth position.

Changements de pied are a simple step like the *soubresauté* but are a development from it as the feet change position once while in the air, as the name suggests. By this development you can see how we are slowly working towards the *entrechats*.

You will start again from good closed fifth position with arms *en bas*. After a *demi-plié*, up into the air. While in the air you change position of the feet once, landing with *demi-plié* back into fifth position. Now the other foot will be in front. Throughout the jump the arms will have been held in a good unstrained position lightly curved in front of the body.

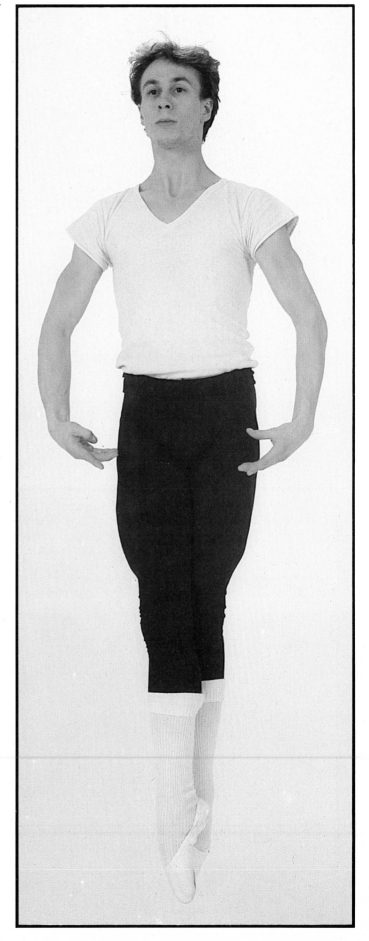

Right: Up into the air keeping a good fifth position so that only one foot is visible from the front.

Far right: The Joffrey Ballet strutting their way through Ruthanna Boris's *Cakewalk* which is made in the pattern of a negro minstrel show.

Pas de Chat

Although this jump is meant to be 'like a cat' I have never seen one actually performing the step. Perhaps you have. It is a jump to the side with the leading leg bent at the knee while in the air. This extends on the way down while the following leg does the same movement. You land back on the ground in the same position as you started. At its highest point, when one leg is on the way to *retiré* and the other on the way down it looks a little like a *demi-plié* in the air while moving sideways, both feet being drawn up under the body.

Suitably enough this step appears in the variation for the White Cat during Aurora's Wedding in *The Sleeping Beauty*. You can also see it used very effectively in Ashton's *Enigma Variations* when Lady Elgar performs

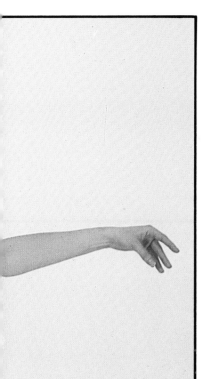

a series while wearing a long Edwardian dress. The sweep of the dress following the movement looks particularly elegant.

To follow the step in sequence. Start in fifth position with arms in third position and the head over the curved arm. Using a *demi-plié* jump to the side bringing the leading (back) leg up to *retiré*. As you start to descend the following leg also comes up to *retiré* as the leading leg begins to extend. You will land back in fifth position with a soft *demi-plié*.

Perhaps if a cat doesn't look exactly like this when it jumps you will at least have noticed the soft grace it has when landing and this is something you should aim for if ever you are performing this step.

Brisé Volé

Your right leg swings forward, starting from *tendu* back and swishing through first position . . .

. . . the left leg being brought up to beat back and front with it *en l'air* . . .

The *brisés* are travelling jumps with a beat included. The beats should be as clean as possible for the audience to see them and should be done well off the floor. This virtuoso step is used in the Bluebird variation, the beats in front and to the back done alternately with the appropriate bird-like *ports de bras*.

Stand on the left foot with the right pointed behind. Swing the right foot through and jump off the left on to the right beating the calves together, landing on the right with a *demi-plié* and the left straight and *en l'air*. Then on through second to back where the right meets it with right straight back and left in *demi-plié*.

The body arcs towards the raised leg in front and to the raised leg behind, but this time looking at it over

the *opposite* shoulder. The right hand does a *ports de bras* to the left leg in front.

This movement derives from stage practice. You will always be seen by the audience, which if you followed the strict classroom rules they would not be able to do.★

★ *As I have already said this is a virtuoso step for professional dancers, so I think that I should again warn you about overstretching yourself while working towards these difficult steps. They are included here as they are an important part of the dancers development but you must be patient and be advised by your teacher on your progress towards them.*

. . . the right leg returning to the ground with a *plié* . . .

. . . while the left leg swings through second to back position . . .

. . . the right leg being raised to beat front and back with it . . .

. . . after which the right foot returns to the ground.

Temps de poisson

We have seen the step like a cat and now we look at a jump like a fish. It is used in a solo for a bird!

This deceptively simple step is extremely difficult to achieve as a great deal of its effect depends on style not an overstretched technique.

It is a high jump; the sort a salmon would do as it leaps out of the water to fight its way upstream. The body arches backwards in the air with the arms above the head (in fifth position *en haut*) and the feet fully stretched back together in fifth position.

The stretching movement should look sleek and elegant in the air, as though you are suspended for a moment at the end of an angler's line.

You will start from fifth position and throughout the leap will keep the feet tightly together. Any separation and the sleek look will be spoiled. It is also important to remember not to train for the curved effect. If you do you will find that you will bend your knees to achieve the curved effect and, apart from looking extremely ugly, this is technically incorrect.

Right: Notice the nice line of the body with no sense of strain. The curved line you are aiming for will not be helped by bending the back or the knees.

Opposite: Yuri Soloviev, one of the best-loved Russian dancers in one of his greatest roles, that of the *Bluebird* in *The Sleeping Beauty*. Although the style of the costume and the make-up appear old-fashioned today, the perfect style is still obvious.

Batterie

This is a group name for all the beaten steps. They are usually done fast and are a development of the *changements* and related steps we performed during the *petit allegro*. It includes the various *entrechat* and the *cabriole* as well as the *brisés*.

In general the sharper and cleaner your leg movements are the more brilliant the step will look.

Entrechat

An *entrechat* is a jump straight up and down with a varying number of changes of the position of the feet. The name of the particular step is related to the number of changes and not to the number of beats.

Having already mastered the *soubresauté* and *changement* you will progress to the *entrechat trois*, *entrechat quatre*, *entrechat cinq*, *entrechat six* and so on. An *entrechat douze* has been recorded but it has little to offer from the point of view of dance.

For an *entrechat six*, start from fifth position with *demi-plié* . . . change the position of your feet twice while in the air . . . and once more before landing with the other foot in front.

The simplest *entrechat* is strictly speaking the *entrechat deux*, but is most commonly referred to as a *royal*.

Starting from fifth position, with appropriate *ports de bras* jump into the air from a smooth *demi-plié*. For an *entrechat quatre* you will start with the right foot in front, then up into the air with the right in front, while in the air move the left foot in front and on the way down move the right foot back in front so that you land in the same position.

An *entrechat six* put simply will mean going up, staying up and changing feet, changing feet again on way down, landing with the opposite foot in front.

The *entrechat* with odd numbers are explained by landing on one foot.

Cabriole

A *cabriole* is a jump with a single or double beat to the front or back. The leading foot is thrown up, the following foot is moved up towards it, beating once or twice before returning to the starting position.

Jetés

We have now reached the big exciting jumps, which always thrill an audience when performed. *Jeté* really means 'to throw' but in ballet the word throw would suggest something too careless and undisciplined. As with all the other steps a good *jeté* must be controlled however carefree it looks to an audience when you are conveying the excitement of a role. It should be a controlled leap cutting cleanly through the air with arms extended into fifth position. Your back must be strongly held and the elevation must be good. No photograph can convey the feeling of power in the *jeté*, the feeling of holding the peak of the jump for a moment before returning to the ground. The elevation, the distance and the soft smooth landing will all depend on the exercises we have already done to develop the *plié* and the small jumps which were planned to give you the bouncing strength of a hard rubber ball. And remember that even the most spectacular jump will be ruined if you don't land gracefully and quietly.

Only with good smooth *ballon*, which literally means the light bouncy quality a dancer should have, can these steps be executed with clarity. In the small jumps the strength and ability to leave the ground came largely from the feet as we have already seen. For these bigger jumps the muscles of the thighs and buttocks will have been brought into play. Your upper body will be held firmly and should not take any real part in projecting yourself, otherwise you will find that the elegant look of the body will be lost.

Above: Eva Evdokimova performing a *jeté en attitude*, a step often seen in ballets by the Danish choreographer Bournonville such as *La Sylphide* or *Napoli*.

Left: Grande jeté en avant.

Grand Écarte

Above: The open *grand écarte* during which the feet should be nicely pointed, even though there is maximum splitting of legs.

The clean splitting of the legs into a wide-open position can also be seen in the *grand écarte* which in general theatre dancing could be referred to as doing the splits! However in the ballet it usually refers to a big jump in which the boy goes straight up into the air, splits his legs wide apart so that they form as near to a straight line as possible. It has only a limited use in the classical ballet, although it is seen to effect in *Les Rendezvous*, and is most frequently found in character dances such as the Russian dances in *The Nutcracker* or *The Sleeping Beauty*.

Fouettés

Start from a single or double pirouette from fifth position, finishing with the working leg in front. It is taken from front through second . . .

. . . and brought sharply into *retiré* position as you turn . . .

This is perhaps the most famous and spectacular step which a ballerina will perform. It is the step which always gets the most applause and it is the step which everyone assumes is the most difficult. This it is, but I think it is always important to stress that it is a step in which the natural element of each ballerina is very important. Some dancers never master it and others can do singles and doubles in any combination with the greatest of ease.

This step takes its name from the French for 'to whip' and this describes what the working leg does, although I should add that in this case the supporting leg is doing a great deal more work than usual. If you consider that the actual 32 turns in the *Black Swan pas de deux* are spectacular it is perhaps easy to forget or not notice that the supporting leg has to do 32 *relevés* onto

point which is a feat in itself!

You can start from an open fourth position to get a good push off or from a *pas de bourrée en tournant* which of course means that the turning movement of your whole body is started before you raise the working leg to begin the circular whipping motion. The raised leg continues to whip around the supporting leg and does not touch the floor during a series of *fouettés*.

The working leg should whip smartly out to second and then back into the knee with a sharp regular rhythm.

The *ports de bras* can vary according to the character of the variation. For instance you may have seen *fouettés* performed with the hands on the hips during *Don Quixote*; attractive but difficult as the body will not have the added momentum of the arms when turning.

Opposite: The two ballerinas prepare for a *fouetté* competition in the London Festival Ballet's production of David Lichine's *Graduation Ball.*

. . . with your head leading as you turn, to find your 'spot' . . .

. . . and back to face the front.

Tours en l'air

This is a jump which will usually be performed by the man and in fact is one of the most used steps in variations. It is a jump turning in the air and landing in the starting position in its simplest form, but of course it is usually a more complicated version, the double *tour en l'air* which you see most often and with a variety of endings depending on the circumstances. Some of the great dancers such as Richard Cragun, have performed triple *tour en l'air* during performance, but it is mostly a matter of academic interest as you will realize that to perform it you must turn so fast that it is difficult to see the three turns!

Starting from fifth position spring into the air through a *demi-plié* for take-off. As you go up your head and eyes will be anticipating the direction you are going and the position in which you will land, rather like the ballerina 'spots' when pirouetting. When anticipating resist a temptation to actually move the head, it should only lead the body around.

When in the air you turn and you will also change the position of the feet before you land softly through a *demi-plié* into a good closed fifth. If of course you are at an advanced stage and are doing a *tour en l'air* as part of an *enchainment* you could land in second position as a linking step.

When you are going up into the air take great care that the **whole** body moves up in a controlled way. Do not hunch the shoulders during the upward movement.

As I have said the good *plié* before and after will ensure a nice soft landing.

While learning the *tour en l'air* the correct *port de bras* will be *en bas*.

From fifth to *temps de cou de pied* . . .

. . . and turn . . .

. . . a *demi-plié* for take off . . .

. . . up into the air, keeping good fifth position . . .

. . . landing with a soft *demi-plié*, . . .

. . . before returning to fifth.

Point Work

While the boys in class go on to work on bigger, more masculine versions of *jetés* and other steps you will see in virtuoso variations, the girls prepare for point work.

Up to now the exercises will have been done on half and three-quarter point in soft shoes. Now you will go on to repeat, on point, some of the basic exercises from the earlier part of the class.

Point work should not start too early. If it does the feet can suffer and become deformed. It will have been reached gradually just as you will have worked towards the more difficult exercises. This part of the centrework will be devoted to strengthening the point technique and I have assumed that you will have worked on preliminary exercises before.

First a mention about shoes and feet in general.

The ideal foot for point work is probably shorter than average and will have a good instep and strong ankles. Exercise can improve both these points. As this is the ideal there will be many variations and perhaps you are one of these! If so it does not mean that you will experience great difficulty. An exaggerated instep may mean that your feet are not so strong, but as consolation they will look prettier. A straighter foot is not so pretty, but it will probably be stronger and a great help in turns and balances.

When you go up on point you must make sure you go square onto the point and not roll onto the side toes. Do not be overcareful which might lead you to be too far back. Do not push over the instep too much. Always take care to keep well turned out and not to 'sickle' which is when the heel of the pointed foot is allowed to stray behind the line of the toe by 'dropping' the ankle. This spoils the line in general and is especially noticeable in *arabesque* or *attitude*.

The shoe you use is also very important and from the earliest days should have been fitted by an expert. Every ballerina knows exactly which shoe suits her foot, but this only follows years of professional experience.

They should fit snugly and tightly, but not so tight as to cramp the toes. You should be sure the ribbon is

Second position on point

Fourth position on point

Fifth position on point

Retiré front under knee

Retiré back, shown from the front.

Retiré back, shown from behind.

attached to the right position and you should learn to tie it firmly, but without in anyway restricting the mobility of your ankle.

A basic exercise before moving on to bigger steps and turns is the *échappe*.

You will start from fifth, do a *demi-plié*, then *relevé* out into second position on point with your legs out an equal distance on both sides before closing back to fifth with the opposite foot in front. You repeat this as many times as your teacher instructs. The number will increase as your strength increases.

Your arms will be in the second position during this exercise.

Other exercises include *retiré passé* which is a development from working equally with both legs as in *echappé* to working with one foot at a time. This exercise is strengthening the point for the clean starting of *pirouettes*.

From fifth position you will *relevé* on to the point of one foot, through *demi-plié* while the other foot is drawn up to a *retiré* position, before returning to fifth position. Of course you will do an equal number of *retiré* with each foot. Your weight will be balanced over the supporting leg.

You can vary the *port de bras* either by raising both arms *en haut* with the upward movement or have the same arm as the raised foot in fifth position with the other arm *en bas*.

A more difficult pose, but very attractive, is the *relévé en arabesque* which you will see in *Les Sylphides* when the ballerina performs a series of them, crossing the stage diagonally. It is also seen in other *pas de deux*, sometimes with the balance *en arabesque* held long for effect.

Above: First *arabesque* on point

Starting from fifth position with right foot in front . . .

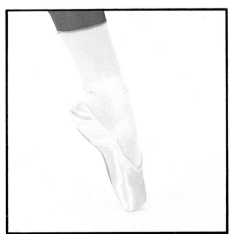

. . . *relevé* up to point on second position . . .

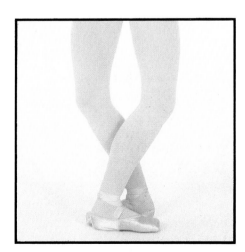

. . . and back down to fifth with the left foot in front.

Double Work

Double work is not really a part of the class we have just been through. When you start work with a partner it will be after a general class such as this, at quite a separate time.

To make your life easy your partner should be well-matched with you, but as you may have noticed during performances life is not always so well arranged so you had better be ready for anything. Small boys have to partner large girls, just as tiny girls may find themselves with a very tall man!

In double work boys take on a great responsibility. They must show the ballerina off to best advantage, never making themselves too obvious. Nevertheless, they must maintain good presence and contribute to the performance. In the great days of the classical ballet at the court of the Tsar the male dancers were called 'porters' as they did little more than carry the ballerina around. Now they are expected to conserve energy to perform a brilliant solo immediately after the *adage*, the slow opening section, of the *pas de deux*.

Double work should start early so that it comes naturally to both dancers and certain positions can be maintained almost without thinking about them. It must be in the boy's range of ability to instinctively hold the ballerina correctly, just as it is to perform a step. There can be no moments of awkwardness when it comes to a performance; no fumbling for the right position.

The number of ways the ballerina will have to be held are limited, although there are a great number of variations on each of these. First she must be supported in a static pose which she could not do by herself without a miracle of balance. The boy can then develop this by turning the ballerina on the spot, which is known as a *promenade*. The ballerina can then *pirouette* on the spot as in the finger *fouetté*, can be then caught in some aerial pose such as a fish dive or be supported in the air in a big lift.

In its simplest form double work can mean the boy lightly holding the ballerina's waist in a *posé arabesque en pointe* which brings a beautiful *arabesque* to greater perfection. The line from finger tip to toe is complemented by the greater elegance of the point over the flat foot.

Above left: Aurora does an unsupported balance *en attitude* with arms *au couronne*.

Left: The prince supports Aurora in an *attitude* balance.

Opposite: An attractive variation of the pose from the *Rose Adage*, with the prince on one knee.

The particular ways of holding hands can vary according to the wishes of the ballerina, but in general when learning she should lay her hand firmly *on* the boy's hand. Too firm a grasp can upset balance as the boy should only support the ballerina's own balance. He is not literally holding her up, other than in emergencies!

You will have seen these *promenades*, indeed the most outstanding and difficult use of them, in the *Rose Adage* in the first act of *The Sleeping Beauty*.

Aurora performs a series of *promenades en attitude* with the four Princes who want to marry her. Between each *promenade*, during which she must hold a good *attitude* with her raised knee pulling towards the opposite shoulder, she holds a perfect balance with arms *au couronne* before taking the hand of the next prince.

In this same dance sequence you will also see Aurora do supported *pirouettes* with the boy standing behind her, his hands lightly supporting her waist. Her partner must know exactly how she is turning for it is quite easy for her to do too many. A good partner will anticipate when to stop or know exactly how to cope by allowing an extra *pirouette* to be completed and not try to force her to a halt.

The ballerina can perform a great number of extra turns if supported this way, just as she can perform finger *fouettés* with her partner behind her, holding on to his middle finger directly above her head.

If the boy holds the girl in this position by the waist and revolves her this is a *promenade*. The boy must walk in a circle close to the ballerina's body, and beware of shuffling inelegantly or pushing the ballerina off point. A variation of this promenade would be if the boy supported the ballerina by holding her outstretched hand and walked around in a big circle, the length of both arms away.

There are no firm rules for the many exciting steps which you will see in *pas de deux* such as *Le Corsaire* with its lifts and throws or the more elegant *The Sleeping Beauty*. Although this is a tender love duet taking place when Aurora marries her Prince, virtuoso steps are cleverly used in it, including the famous fish dives. In the music there is a great preparation for the step so it should not come as a surprise. And yet it always does.

The Prince does a preparation before resting in open fourth position which will give him greater stability and movability from back to front when the girl falls forward in his arm.

The ballerina runs, *pirouettes*, and is caught around the waist by the Prince as she does so. He then tips her forward over his left knee while her outstretched hand almost sweeps the floor. Her body makes an elegant upswept line.

At the end of the *pas de deux* a variation of this is used when Aurora is caught round the waist, and put into 'fish' position over the Prince's knee. By bending one knee behind his back Aurora lies apparently unsupported across his body.

Only much practice and a close understanding between the performers can bring these moves to perfection. Only practice and understanding can make sure that they are performed in a tasteful way and not turned into party tricks.

Opposite: Supported *arabesque*.

Above left: Supported *arabesque*, during which the ballerina will often do a *promenade*, in other words be slowly pirouetted by her partner.

Left: A *pressage* lift of which you will see many variations such as when the girl brings her foot up to a *retiré* position.

Above left : For a finger *fouetté* the girl brings her leg up to *retiré* . . .

Above right : . . . takes it straight out in front . . .

Right : . . . whips it back through second to *retiré* causing the turn.
At the same time her raised hand loosely grasps the boy's finger directly
above her head.

Left: For this fish dive, Ashley has caught Angela around her waist after she has made a single *pirouette*, maintaining a good line with his free arm. You can see that Angela's body is in a nice natural curve, without bent knees; the same sort of curve you have already seen in the *temps de poisson*, but tipped over so that the head is lower than the feet.

Below: Rudolf Nureyev and Patricia Ruanne perform a fish dive in the Aurora *pas de deux* during the wedding celebrations in Act III of Nureyev's production of *The Sleeping Beauty*.

Costume

In many of the ballets you will see today, particularly the very modern ones, dancers often wear only body tights, much the same as those you will wear for your classes. We accept this as perfectly natural, but it would have totally shocked audiences at the very earliest dance performances in the fifteenth and sixteenth centuries.

At that time it would have been unthinkable for a lady dancer, who would have been a court lady and not a paid performer, to show even a hint of her ankle. It was a long time before any lady would be allowed to dance professionally at all, just as the women's parts were played by boys in Shakespeare's plays. The noblemen could dance more freely as their everyday costume included tights, but even they had rather cumbersome short skirts. They could perform some more intricate footwork because of this, but the ladies in their stiff hooped skirts, tight bodices and extremely elaborate hairstyles could do little more than graceful walking. The dances of that time would make their effect by the elaborate costumes, the ornately decorated floats and carriages which carried the singers and the complicated floor patterns.

If an effect of flight was required the dancer could not jump, but would be hauled up and down by com-plicated machinery. Gods and goddesses would appear through trapdoors or on wires.

We know almost exactly when the first changes in costume were made. The first true ballerina to dance in a slightly shortened skirt was Marie de Camargo and she was immortalized in the famous paintings by Lancret, one of which is in London in the Wallace Collection. In it you can see her feet and just a hint of ankle. You can also see the effect this had on the musicians playing for her. One is concentrating much more on her twinkling feet than on his music. She was credited with performing the first *entrechat* and was generally noted for her footwork. To show this off her hem had to be raised, but it would be another fifty years before the skirt was raised much more. The other great ballerina of the day, Marie Sallé, also tried hard to change the restriction costumes when she danced the ballet *Pygmalion* dressed in a flowing Greek tunic which suited the subject. However, she was not able

Below: Ballet Theatre Contemporain in one of their modern works.

Opposite: A scene from Act II of Festival Ballet's production of *Giselle*.

to do this in Paris and had to give her performances in London.

A great breakthrough in dance dress came with the invention of tights which is usually attributed to Maillot, the costume master at the Paris Opera. With these under lighter costumes the dancer was not really naked, although it took some time for even these to be accepted. The Pope only grudgingly allowed them, but insisted that they should be blue!

By the beginning of the nineteenth century and the arrival of the Romantic ballet a costume had been devised which was to become a standard dress for the ballerina; the long romantic tutu, with its bell-shaped skirt cut just below the knee, a fitted bodice and perhaps some light tulle covering around the shoulders. To this day you can see it in ballets such as *Giselle* and *La Sylphide* which date from this period and in *Les Sylphides* created nearly eighty years later.

Following the Romantic era ballets such as *Coppelia* and *Don Quixote* introduced colourful national costumes into ballet and at the same time often allowed ballerinas to appear on stage in tight fitting trousers. As technique progressed and the ballerina became completely dominant the shorter classical tutu came into use to show off the brilliant steps.

As ballet emerged into the twentieth century costume design went many different ways. For the romantic and classical ballets designers stayed true to the style in which they were created. For the new ballets created by choreographers freed from the restrictions of court etiquette or the wishes of emperors, designers were free to do exactly what they wanted.

Today, with ballet a wide popular art, the dancers costume is kept to a minimum so that the beautiful steps and poses can be appreciated by the audience.

Opposite: Ballerinas of London Festival Ballet in *Etudes*.

Below: La Camargo painted by Lancret.

The Choreographer

Of all the names you see on a programme at the ballet that of the choreographer should be the most important. The ballerina may be more famous and the conductor very important, but it is the choreographer who will have had the idea for the ballet, created the steps, arranged for the design of costumes and scenery and perhaps even commissioned the music.

Of course it is possible on some occasions that he will only be responsible for arranging the steps, whether he is working in the ballet, on a big musical or on a dance for the television. The most important American choreographer, George Balanchine, once choreographed the steps for some circus elephants.

In the sixteenth century this would not have seemed odd, as the entertainments which the travelling dancers created often included complicated dances for horses and riders, rather like carnivals or circuses today.

Originally choreography meant the writing down of dances by the dancing or ballet master who created them. Today the ballet master is the person who takes dancers in their daily classes, helps arrange the schedule of a busy ballet company and tries to keep them in fine form as well as teaching dancers their roles.

This gradual change of name from ballet master to choreographer has come about only recently. We talk of a great choreographer such as Marius Petipa, creator of the greatest classical ballets, but he really held the official post of Ballet Master at the Tsar's Imperial Ballet in St Petersburg (now Leningrad).

The work of the choreographer today can be divided into two equally important parts. He must do the creative work of inventing different *enchâinments* and an original as well as organizing the work of his collaborators, the designers, musicians and lighting technicians.

Ideally he should be able to blend all these things into one successful production, but if one part has to be weaker than the rest, I think we would all be happier with original steps and not-so-good decor than the other way round. In many ways this is a more difficult job than that of a film director who has similar responsibilities, but does not have to write the story or train the actors.

There are as many ways for the choreographer to start work on a ballet as there are ballets. If he is asked to produce a new version of a great classic such as *Swan Lake* he already has the well-known story and the wonderful music. He can, however, rearrange these and

Above: Rudolf Nureyev and Patricia Ruanne in *The Sleeping Beauty.*

Left: The great American choreographer George Balanchine rehearsing.

74

keep only a little of the original choreography which has been handed down to us by other dancers or by notation. Even very original versions of *Swan Lake* include the famous lakeside scene, but with a ballet such as *The Nutcracker* there is very little of the original left; only the great *pas de deux* for the Sugar Plum Fairy and the Nutcracker Prince.

If the choreographer is asked to produce an original work for a company he may already have some music in mind to inspire him or he may once have been told a story which he thought would make a good ballet. In this case he might ask a composer to write some music specially for him or simply take the advice of his conductor about a piece of existing music.

A lot of the greatest music was written to order. Marius Petipa sent Tchaikovsky very detailed notes about his requirements for *The Sleeping Beauty* and *The Nutcracker*. Although he would request 'four bars with a chord of astonishment' for the giving out of presents or 'six bars for the squeaking of mice' it did not stop Tchaikovsky producing a glorious score.

It would seem important to have the music before starting work on the steps, but this is not necessary. Many ballets have been made while the music was being written and one ballet *The Young Man and Death*, recently recreated for Baryshnikov, was originally rehearsed to jazz but at the last minute performed to a very powerful piece by Bach.

Dancers have often inspired choreographers by the way they move or by their personalities. Frederick Ashton has created many wonderful ballets for Margot Fonteyn and Kenneth Macmillan found that Lynn

Right: Two designs for costumes for *The Nutcracker* by the Russian Alexander Benois.

Below: Brian Shaw rehearsing with Ashley and Angela.

Seymour was his perfect ballerina. Both of these choreographers have used the personalities of the dancers as well as their dance talent; Fonteyn's charm as the water spirit in *Ondine* dancing with her own shadow and Seymour's great dramatic talent as the innocent child in *The Invitation*. George Balanchine is inspired by a type of dancer; a special type we now even refer to as a 'Balanchine dancer', usually having long legs with high extensions, such as Suzanne Farrell.

The way the choreographer goes about creating the actual steps varies as greatly as his inspiration. Some plan very carefully at home, writing notes or even making little drawings of groups of dancers. Some, such as Balanchine, rely almost entirely on detailed study of the music for their inspiration. The real work, however, must still be done in the studio with the dancers and often their contribution is overlooked. Accidents, too, can play their part. In one famous case an accident was kept in the ballet as a natural move. When George Balanchine was making *Serenade* one of the girls tripped and fell as the *corps de ballet* was running from the stage. It became a moving moment in the final version of this glorious pure dance work.

Away from the studio much of the choreographer's time must go into planning the large scale crowd scenes for dancers or non-dancing extras. He must organize the fight scenes for a ballet, such as *Romeo and Juliet*, or worry about special scenic effects, such as the sudden magical disappearances of the Sylph in *La Sylphide*.

After choosing a designer the choreographer will first see sketches of costumes and scenery and will suggest any little alterations he may think necessary; a skirt too long, stairs too steep or not enough space for the big crowd scenes. A model will be made of the scenery for the technicians and painters to work from and samples of material will be pinned to the costume sketches to guide the wardrobe. There will be boring sessions of costume fittings for the dancers while costumes are pinned and unpinned, seams tried for strength or sleeves and legs for freedom of movement. This can be a particularly trying time for the *corps de ballet* who may have three or four changes of costume in a big production such as *The Sleeping Beauty* or *Swan Lake*. They may be peasant girls in the first act, swans in the second, court ladies in the third act and back to being swans for the last. Not every company has enough dancers to make sure a swan stays a swan for a whole evening! Not only will these changes involve costume. There will also be suitable changes of makeup and hair style. The peasant girl will have flowers in her

hair, the swan a classical drawn-back style with feathers and the court lady an elaborate wing.

While the choreographer, designer and dancers have been getting on with their work, the conductor will have been arranging the music and rehearsing the orchestra. Often a well-known classic which the orchestra have played many times can prove more difficult than a very complicated piece of ultra-modern music. It must be fresh and lively and the tempi must be adjusted to suit each different ballerina and soloist. One will want her variation fast, another slow. The conductor will have attended rehearsals and perhaps have played the piano for some of them, marking his score with cuts, changes of tempo, repeats or pauses. Small things which will not be noticed during the performance must be meticulously rehearsed. One Prince will want to start his solo on stage, another may want to start in the wings and the conductor must be warned about this to avoid awkward pauses. In some performances of the *The Nutcracker* you may have noticed that the Sugar Plum Fairy starts her famous tinkling variation on stage; in others she starts off-stage.

All these parts of the production come together for the first time at the first stage rehearsal and things can prove chaotic. Dancers may find that costumes aren't so comfortable to dance in; a real door or staircase will prove more difficult to cope with than chalk marks on a studio floor; actual props such as crossbows or bouquets can prove cumbersome and new shoes may be less comfortable than the old ballet shoes used during rehearsals. After weeks of rehearsing to a piano the full

orchestral version of unfamiliar music can come as a surprise and the tempo may not be right or important cues missed. Rarely does such a rehearsal go straight through without a lot of stopping and starting.

The choreographer, with his technical stage director, must preside over this monster jigsaw puzzle and attempt to fit all the pieces into their right place in time for that all-important first night.

Six ballets

Going to the ballet can be a history lesson as well as entertainment. Ballets from the very earliest years of dancing as a theatrical art, when it broke away from being a court entertainment, are danced by most companies around the world and it is also possible to find at least one ballet from each later period as well.

The six ballets on the following pages are chosen for their place in ballet history and their popularity.

La Fille Mal Gardée represents two stages in ballet history as it has been revived several times in different periods. It was originally created before *Giselle* which represents the Romantic period, but also has much in common with ballets such as *Coppelia* which followed. *Swan Lake* and *The Nutcracker* are two of three great classic ballets and *Petrouchka* brings us into the twentieth century and the start of the movement of ballet throughout the world. *Romeo and Juliet*, a timeless story, shows the way the large-scale full length ballet developed in Russia after the Revolution and in the renewing of that tradition in the West.

La Fille Mal Gardée

Right: Lise and Colas (Brenda Last and Desmond Kelly) steal a kiss while poor Alain is distracted by Lise's friends.

A ballet with this title and story was first created in 1789 by Dauberval in Bordeaux. It is important in ballet history as it was the first major work to show ordinary people going about their everyday business. Before this, dance had been more concerned with gods and goddesses and classical themes.

Not only were the people real, but the story was carefully worked out and the drama shown in dance. Similar characters would reappear in later ballets of the following period, such as the German peasants in the first act of *Giselle* or the Scottish crofters in *La Sylphide*.

The steps and music of the original version are lost. The delightful story with its wit and humour, however, has been retained to charm us today.

The story

Lise lives with her mother, the Widow Simone, on a farm in France. She is in love with a young farmer, Colas, but her mother has other, more ambitious, plans for her. Poor Colas has to sneak in and out of the farm to see Lise and usually ends up being chased off by Widow Simone in a hail of plant pots.

In one of the few moments they manage to have together they show their love for one another and tie a very pretty love knot with the ribbon Colas has left on the barn door as a sign to Lise.

This time Widow Simone is more than ever determined to chase him off her property as she is expecting their rich neighbour, Farmer Thomas, and his simpleton son, Alain. She sends Lise into the farmhouse to put on her prettiest dress as she has plans to arrange for her to marry Alain. Lise obeys her mother unwillingly and sits unhappily watching Alain entertain them, dancing with his umbrella, to which he is very attached.

Luckily it is soon time to go to the harvesting; Lise and Widow Simone by pony trap followed by Lise's friends and Colas who brings wine.

Once in the fields it is easier for the two lovers to meet while Widow Simone enjoys a picnic with Farmer Thomas. They are able to join in the general dancing and to entertain their friends. Alain, too, wants to dance with Lise. She lets him, but he is so simple he does not realize that Colas is joining in and stealing kisses while he concentrates too hard on partnering her.

After joining the harvesters in a maypole dance they manage to escape together into the woods. Widow Simone notices that they are missing, but she is distracted by Lise's friends who beg her to dance for them. Eager to show off she soon forgets the missing lovers.

A storm breaks out and the workers scatter leaving Colas and Lise for a brief moment together before Widow Simone drags her daughter home.

Once in their spacious farm-house they dry themselves off and Widow Simone puts a scarf on Lise to ward off chills. She also firmly locks the door to keep Lise in and Colas out. When she falls asleep she does not know that Colas is able to greet Lise over the top of the door, but she does know when Lise tries to take the keys from her pocket.

After the harvesters have brought in some wheat to dry and to collect their pay the Widow goes out, locking the door firmly behind her. Lise is left alone to dream about her future with Colas and the family they will have. As she is pretending to care for their children Colas jumps out from under the wheat. Lise is horrified when she realizes that he was able to see what she was doing, but he soon manages to calm her and show that he shares her dreams. They exchange scarves, but as they do so they hear Widow Simone returning. In panic Colas tries to hide in a drawer, under the table, up the chimney. Lise hides him in her bedroom.

Always suspicious, widow Simone notices the different scarf Lise is wearing, but before she can really find out whether or not Coles got into the house, Farmer Thomas and Alain arrive with the village Notary and his clerk to sign the marriage agreement. Widow Simone orders Lise to her bedroom to change. She does not understand why Lise is reluctant to go, but is too concerned about the marriage contract to think twice about it. Up the stairs Lise goes and is locked into the room for good measure.

When the contract is signed, Widow Simone gives Alain the keys to Lise's room. He coyly mounts the stairs to claim his bride, but on unlocking the door finds her in Colas' arms.

The Widow swears never to forgive her daughter as she can see a fortune being lost when Farmer Thomas storms out taking the sad, simple Alain with him.

Lise's friends beg Widow Simone to relent, which she does when she sees that Lise and Colas are truly in love. There is joyous dancing and singing out into the farmyard.

When all is quiet Alain returns to claim his precious umbrella; forgotten in his moment of distress.

The choreographers

Dauberval who created the original version broke new ground when he put into practice the ideas of his teacher, Noverre. The story was used again by Jean Aumer at the Paris Opèra in 1828, with new music by Hérold. This is the music you will recognize in the production by Frederick Ashton which is danced by many companies, including the Royal Ballet in the United Kingdom, the National Ballet of Canada and the Australian Ballet.

Yet another version was produced in 1864 with more new music by Hertel and it was this music which Marius Petipa and Lev Ivanov used for the production of 1885 and which is the basis of productions today in Russia, as well as by American Ballet Theater.

Frederick Ashton, the most English choreographer, was actually born in Ecuador and decided to become a dancer after seeing Pavlova dance in Peru. When he came to London he studied with Massine and Marie Rambert, who had worked in Paris with Nijinsky and was one of the founders of the British Ballet. With the encouragement of Rambert he was able to start choreographing very early and by the middle of the 1930s had already created ballets such as *Façade* and *Les Rendezvous* which you can still see today. He had also started to work with the young Margot Fonteyn and went on to create her greatest triumphs.

He created *La Fille Mal Gardée* in 1960 and became Director of the Royal Ballet in 1963. Since his retirement from that position in 1970 he has made beautiful lyrical ballets for Antoinette Sibley and Anthony Dowell as well as the funny and charming film *The Tales of Beatrix Potter*, in which he also danced as Mrs Tiggy-winkle.

Brian Shaw as the Widow Simone in the last act of *La Fille Mal Garde*.

Giselle

Right: Eva Evdokimova as *Giselle* is crowned queen of the vine harvest in Mary Skeaping's production for London Festival Ballet.

The story of the peasant girl, Giselle, is one of the most popular and most performed ballets still danced.

It is the most important ballet from the Romantic period, which lasted for only about twenty years from 1830, when the subjects always concerned ethereal magical beings such as the Wilis in *Giselle* or the Sylphs in *La Sylphide*.

Giselle was first produced in Paris in 1841 nine years after *La Sylphide* which had been created for the greatest Romantic ballerina, Marie Taglioni. The first Giselle was Carlotta Grisi, who also danced the first performance in London in 1842 and the music (except the famous *Peasant pas de deux*) was by Adolphe Adam.

The story

Giselle, a simple peasant girl, lives with her mother in a small cottage in a clearing in the forest. She is loved by one of the villagers, a gamekeeper called Hilarion, who brings her gifts of pheasants killed in the woods.

Unfortunately Giselle has met and fallen in love with someone she knows only as Loys. He is really Prince Albrecht escaping from the rich life of court to a more simple existence. Hilarion is very jealous and by chance sees Albrecht arrive in the village wearing his cape and sword. He remembers where Albrecht hides them, as he is sure that through these clues he will find out his true identity.

Giselle loves to dance and during the celebrations of the vine harvest, when she is crowned queen, she dances with Albrecht. Her mother warns her of the dangers of straining herself and the sad consequences. As an extra warning she tells Giselle and the assembled villagers the legend of the Wilis who haunt the forest. They are the ghosts of girls who die before their wedding day and they take terrible revenge on any man they find in their domain after nightfall.

Soon after these celebrations a royal hunting party arrives at the village for rest and refreshment. Albrecht's servant has warned him of their arrival and he hides. Hilarion sees this as the chance to reveal Albrecht's identity, after he has compared the crest on the royal hunting horn with that on Albrecht's sword. He makes Albrecht confront the royal party who are surprised to see him there, especially his bethrothed, Bathilde.

Giselle cannot believe it when Bathilde tells her that she is engaged to Albrecht and insists that they are to wed. When it is made clear to her that Bathilde is right, Giselle is distraught. She does not know what to do and grabs the sword in a vain attempt to kill herself. She relieves moments of happiness with Albrecht, even the moment when he proved he loved her by counting the petals on a flower. She was not to know that he had cheated them. The strain of the shock takes its toll and she rushes into her mother's arms where she dies.

After Giselle has been buried deep in the forest she is welcomed into the ranks of the Wilis by Myrtha, their ruthless queen. She hears the sound of someone approaching and orders the Wilis away into the forest. It is Hilarion coming in grief to the grave. Unsuspecting he kneels at the grave only to be surprised by the Wilis and forced to a terrible death. Albrecht, too, brings flowers to the grave and feels the presence of Giselle to be near. She appears to him, but he does not know if she is real or just in his imagination as she floats around him. His dream is interrupted by Myrtha and the Wilis and he is commanded to dance to death. Giselle pleads for him and tries to protect him near the cross on her grave, but to no avail. Myrtha is unrelenting, but Giselle manages to sustain Albrecht until dawn is near and the power of the Wilis fades. Giselle too fades away leaving him crumpled flowers to remind him of her love.

The choreographers

The choreography of this ballet still uses much of the original version. Of course, as technique developed there was greater use of point work and different choreographers over the years have added their own steps.

The original choreography was credited to Coralli, but as the first Giselle was Carlotta Grisi it is possible that many of her dances were created by her own teacher, Perrot. While the ballet was not often performed in the West during the nineteenth century it was kept alive by Marius Petipa in Russia where he first danced it.

Of many modern versions that of Mary Skeaping for London Festival Ballet is the most successful. Mary Skeaping danced with Anna Pavlova's company and later became ballet mistress of the Sadler's Wells Ballet and Director of the Royal Swedish Ballet. She is most famous for her research into court dances of the eighteenth century and has created period dances for many famous films, such as *Anne of a Thousand Days*, where historical dances and choreography are required.

Left: Giselle and Albrecht in their pas de deux during Act II of *Giselle*. Although commanded to dance with Albrecht until he dies, Giselle outwits Myrtha by sustaining him until dawn breaks and with it the power of the Wilis.

The Nutcracker

Right: Herr Drosselmeyer
produces a doll to amuse the
children at their Christmas party
during Act I of *The Nutcracker.*

Clara and her Nutcracker Prince appear on the stage perhaps more than any other ballet characters. This Christmas favourite was first performed in St Petersburg (now Leningrad) on December 18th 1892. Just like *Swan Lake* it was not a great success and it is difficult now for us to realize that the audiences, who were used to very simple ballet music, found Tchaikovsky's beautiful music difficult to understand.

The Nutcracker was performed fifteen years after the first production of *Swan Lake*, but three years before the successful version we know now. Most of the original choreography has been lost, but the charming Christmas tale continues to delight audiences.

The story

Mayor Stahlbaum is giving a Christmas Eve party for his children, Clara and Fritz. Their friends arrive with their parents and also a mysterious visitor bringing unusual gifts.

He is Herr Drosselmeyer, and he produces a Nutcracker Doll for Clara, who has also been given ballet shoes. Fritz gets a soldier's uniform and he and his friends terrorize the girls, even breaking Clara's doll. Drosselmeyer soon mends it and also produces dancing dolls to entertain the children.

After the excitement of the party and the fine food the guests leave and Clara and Fritz go to bed. Clara is unsettled and can't sleep. She comes down to the drawing room to see her doll in its box beneath the Christmas tree. As she bends over it Drosselmeyer suddenly appears and makes the Christmas tree grow magically. As it does he also makes the doll come alive. The Nutcracker and his soldiers are attacked by hordes of mice led by the evil Mouse King. During the battle the Nutcracker falls and the Mouse King moves in to kill him. Thinking quickly, Clara takes off one of her ballet slippers and throws it at him. As the Mouse King is surprised the Nutcracker is able to regain the advantage and kill him. Drosselmeyer then transforms the Nutcracker into a handsome prince who takes Clara on a magical journey.

They travel through the Land of Snow, meeting the Snow Queen and her sweeping, swirling Snowflakes, and then on to the Land of Sweets. Clara meets the Sugar Plum Fairy and after the Prince tells how Clara saved him the Sugar Plum Fairy orders a grand *divertissement* of the sweets in her honour. There is a coffee dance from Arabia and a tea dance from China. Madame Bonbonière produces her little polichinelles from under her voluminous skirt and there is the beautiful Waltz of the Flowers. The Prince and the Sugar Plum Fairy do their very grand *pas de deux* but on the arrival of Drosselmeyer with her Nutcracker Doll the Sweets and Flowers fade away.

Mayor and Mrs Stahlbaum anxiously come into the drawing room to look for Clara. They find her fast asleep beneath the tree holding her beloved doll. She looks very contented as though she is having the most marvellous dream.

The choreographers

Marius Petipa planned the production in great detail with Tchaikovsky, but then fell ill. As a result his assistant, Lev Ivanov, was given the task of creating the actual steps. He had always been kept very much in the background and at times Petipa had even taken credit for his work. On this occasion his great lyrical talent and musicality were fully recognized.

Since that time there have been countless productions of *The Nutcracker* from the most modest ballet school to the grand production by Rudolph Nureyev. Perhaps the most entertaining today is that by George Balanchine for New York City Ballet.

George Balanchine is more famous for the ballets he has created in the neo-classical style of which he is the supreme master. But when he set out to create *The Nutcracker* he remembered his days as a student in the Imperial School in St Petersburg and the air of wonder it had. His production is full of magical moments which include the biggest Christmas tree on any stage and a special effect which enables the Sugar Plum Fairy to glide across the stage in *arabesque* as though on ice.

When Balanchine left Russia he joined the Diaghilev company as dancer and choreographer. After Diaghilev's death he worked in France and England before being invited to America. His early efforts there have now grown into the School of American Ballet and the New York City Ballet. This is how ballet develops. The style we call 'American' is in direct line through one person to the teaching of the Imperial School at the time of the death of Petipa.

Some of Balanchine's most famous ballets over a period of forty years were made in close collaboration with another Russian, the composer Igor Stravinsky, whose music caused such an outcry in Paris in the early years of the century.

The set design for Festival Ballet's production of *The Nutcracker*.

Merle Park and Rudolf Nureyev in the grand *pas de deux* from the Royal Ballet's production of *The Nutcracker*.

Swan Lake

The story of the ballet *Swan Lake* is perhaps the best known of all. What isn't so well known is that the ballet was not a success when it was first produced in Moscow in 1877. This first production used the Tchaikovsky music, but rearranged in a very unsatisfactory way. It had different choreography which was reported as being very ordinary. Although it was kept in the Moscow repertory for some time it was not until nearly twenty years later that the production we know came about. Even this was only because *The Sleeping Beauty* was a success and we can be fairly certain that without *The Sleeping Beauty* we might not today have *Swan Lake*.

In most peoples mind *Swan Lake* **is** ballet. The strong image of the swan was used later by Michael Foline for Anna Pavlova in *The Dying Swan*, which of course has no connection with *Swan Lake*.

The story

Prince Siegfried is celebrating his coming of age in the palace grounds. His retainers bring him gifts and he dances with the peasant girls. His mother brings her present, too; a magnificent jewelled crossbow. She also tells him that as he is now of age he is expected to marry. A ball will be arranged to which all the eligible princesses will be invited and Siegfried will have to choose his bride. He is not happy about this, but his mother insists. While brooding over this difficult position Siegfried sees a flight of swans overhead and calls his retainers to go to the forest with him.

Once in the forest at the side of a lake Siegfried sees the most beautiful swan. As he takes aim to shoot he is astonished as it leaves the lake and takes the form of a woman. He lays down his crossbow and approaches her, but she is frightened. She tells him that she is Odette, a princess taken from her home by the evil magician, von Rothbart, and transformed into a swan to keep her in his power. Only someone swearing true love can break the spell. Siegfried is moved by her story and taken by her beauty falls in love with her. Their tender duet is interrupted by von Rothbart who puts Odette back under his spell.

At the ball to choose a bride Siegfried thinks only of Odette and will not make a choice. His mother is annoyed, but then a fanfare of trumpets heralds an unexpected guest. It is von Rothbart disguised as a merchant and he has brought with him his daughter Odile, cleverly pretending to be Odette. Fooled by Odile's disguise and her guile when she dances with him, Siegfried tells his mother that this is the person he wants

to marry. He does not see Odette fluttering helplessly outside the tall windows. Once Siegfried has expressed his intention, von Rothbart takes the opportunity to make him swear eternal love to Odile. Siegfried, completely under her spell, does so willingly. His vow to Odette has been broken. Von Rothbart and Odile leave triumphantly, while Siegfried, realizing his mistake, rushes headlong to the forest.

Odette is at the lakeside surrounded by the other swans. Siegfried finds her and expresses his sorrow at his foolishness and begs her to believe that he truly loves her. Odette knows it is too late and that she is now in von Rothbart's power for ever. In desperation they throw themselves into the lake and in defying von Rothbart they destroy him by the power of their love. They are united for ever in eternity.

Left: The lakeside scene from *Swan Lake* with Natalie Bessmertnova as Odette and Mikhael Lavrosky as Siegfried.

Below: During Act III of *Swan Lake*, set in the castle ballroom, Siegfried (Lavrosky) meets Odile, the Black Swan (Bessmertnova) whom he believes to be his beloved Odette.

The choreographers

Marius Petipa was the main force behind the Imperial Ballet in St Petersburg for over 50 years. He was the master of the great spectacle, as in the magnificent court scenes of *The Sleeping Beauty*. He could also arrange cleverly the dances for the different degrees of ballerina in the company. Each would expect to dance precisely the solo her position demanded almost as film stars today are very careful about their billing on a poster.

After his illness during the production of *The Nutcracker*, which had given Lev Ivanov his golden opportunity, Petipa divided up the work on *Swan Lake* in the wisest possible way. He created the court scenes of the first and third acts while the 'white' acts, the second and fourth were to be created by Ivanov.

Petrouchka

Above: The Charlatan calls the crows to see his sideshow.

Below: After attacking the Moor, Petrouchka is thrown into his cell

This colourful ballet with its liveliness and bustle also has sad overtones. It is one of the ballets most closely connected to Vaslav Nijinsky, the greatest male dancer of the age. He played the part of the cruelly treated puppet with such pathos that it reminds us of his own sad fate. After a dancing career of just ten years, during which he created a legend, he lived on for another 33 years under the shadow of mental illness. He died in London in 1950.

Petrouchka was one of the earliest ballets created by Mikhail Fokine under the guidance of Serge de Diaghilev. These talented people felt that they had to leave their homeland as they were not allowed to create the sort of ballets they wanted to. They made their base in Paris and from this company modern ballet grew.

The story

During the Butterweek Fair in St Petersburg a mysterious showman sets up his sideshow, surrounded by the busy stalls, street dancers, nurses and coachmen. At the height of the activity he calls the people to his show to see his wonderful puppets.

The curtains part revealing the Moor, the Ballerina and the sad figure of Petrouchka. They dance for the crowd in their places and in front of the stall. It seems that Petrouchka has almost human feelings and is in love with the slightly silly Ballerina. She in turn is more interested in the Moor.

After the show the puppets return to their booths. As the fair continues outside, the three puppets inside continue their relationship. The ballerina taunts Petrouchka and then leaves him to visit the stupid Moor who is amusing himself playing with a coconut. However when Petrouchka follows her into his cell he becomes insanely jealous and chases him out with his scimitar.

The crowd outside see the signs of the commotion within the side show and are amazed when the dolls rush out; Petrouchka pursued by the Moor and the Ballerina. The Moor strikes Petrouchka to the ground. People run for the police. The crowd gather round the body horrified. But the Showman lifts up the lifeless body and shows them that it is indeed just a doll. They leave satisfied as night draws in and the fair closes. The Showman cleans up and tidies his stall, but as he leaves the fairground for the night the figure of Petrouchka is seen over the sideshow in a terrifying and horrifying mocking gesture.

The choreographer

Michael Fokine was born in St Petersburg in 1880. He became a dancer in the Imperial Theatre and in his early twenties began to choreograph. In 1907 he created the *Dying Swan* for Anna Pavlova and was soon working with Diaghilev and making preparations for their first tour to Paris. During the next five years he created such ballets as *Les Sylphides*, *The Firebird* and *Scheherazade*. When he left the Diaghilev company he returned to Russia, but like so many of his countrymen was cut off from his homeland by the Revolution in 1917.

In *Petrouchka* he worked with Igor Stravinsky who was to become such an important composer of music for the ballet, and who eventually would become strongly identified with George Balanchine and American ballet. His music was regarded as outrageously modern when first written, in particular the score he was to write for Nijinsky's *The Rite of Spring*. There was such a riot in the theatre at the first performance that dancers could not hear the music and Nijinsky had to stand in the wings shouting the musical counts to them so that they could carry on.

Top: The three puppets dance for the crowd.

Above: The stupid Moor amuses himself by playing with a coconut.

Romeo and Juliet

Right: Rudolf Nureyev as Romeo in Kenneth MacMillan's production for the Royal Ballet. The part of Juliet was first danced by Margot Fonteyn and set the seal on a partnership between the two dancers which enthralled everyone who saw them dance together.

After the death of Diaghilev in 1929 the many very talented people he had gathered around him scattered about the world to find themselves work. Some became teachers in Australia and New Zealand, others all over America. Some stayed in Europe and many important people came to Britain. Few returned to their native Russia, but one who did was the composer Prokofiev.

Inside Russia the classical ballet did not develop, as it had too many connections with the Tsar's regime. The strong teaching tradition, however, continued and produced such great dancers as Ulanova.

When Prokofiev was finally able to get his idea for a ballet based on Shakespeare's *Romeo and Juliet* accepted it was Ulanova who would be the first Juliet in Russia and she too danced the role when the Bolshoi Ballet finally visited London over fifteen years later, in 1956.

In most of the balletic versions of the story many of the details of Shakespeare's tragedy have been omitted and we concentrate on the central, great but touching drama.

The story

The families of Montagu and Capulet in Verona have long been enemies. Romeo, son of the Montagus, and his friends Mercutio and Benvolio, spend their days in the market place pursuing their loves or teasing the trades people. They have an argument with Tybalt, Juliet's brother, which leads to a serious fight. Both Lord Montagu and Lord Capulet join in, with their retainers, until the Prince of Verona commands them to stop. He further commands that they heal the rift between the houses.

The Capulets give a very grand ball and allow their young daughter, Juliet, to attend. Her parents have promised her in marriage to Paris, a young nobleman with whom she shyly dances at the ball.

Romeo and his friends sneak into the house, masked to avoid recognition. This prank has serious results for Romeo sees Juliet for the first time. He instantly falls in love with her and it is clear that she, too, has seen someone she can love. Tybalt recognizes Romeo and orders him to leave, but Lord Capulet, remembering the Prince's order, allows him to stay.

At night, unable to sleep, Juliet goes out onto her balcony thinking only of Romeo. He appears in the garden below and they express their love for one another.

Romeo is now determined that he will marry Juliet, and a letter from her, delivered by her nurse, tells him that she will become his wife.

They secretly meet at the small chapel of Friar Lawrence who marries them, hoping that this bond will unite their families in harmony.

When Romeo returns to the town he finds that his friends are again fighting with Tybalt. He tries to stop the fight, but Tybalt mistakes this for cowardice and carries on fighting. He kills Mercutio. In anger Romeo takes a sword and retaliates by killing Tybalt, for which he is banished by the Prince. He spends one last night with Juliet and leaves Verona at dawn.

Juliet is woken by her nurse with the news that her parents are bringing Paris to her so that he may formally ask for her hand in marriage. Juliet refuses, in spite of terrible threats from her father.

Desolate, she resolves that her only hope is to ask Friar Lawrence for his help. He gives her a potion which will make her fall into a death-like sleep. When she has been placed in the family vault Friar Lawrence will arrange for Romeo to come and take her away.

So that her family will not suspect she has a plan she agrees to marry Paris, but then takes the potion. When the nurse and her friends arrive with her wedding dress they find her apparently dead and the phial of poison near her hand.

The family place her in the deep vault where she lies waiting for Romeo. But the message about the secret potion does not reach Romeo and he believes that she is really dead. He comes to the vault and poisons himself at her side. Slowly the Friar's potion wears off and Juliet regains consciousness only to find Romeo dead. Horrified, she kills herself.

The choreographers

The Russian version of the ballet was created by Leonide Lavrovsky, father of the famous dancer with the Bolshoi Ballet, Mikhail Lavrovsky. The sumptuous production made an equally successful film which has been widely shown.

Other important versions of this ballet include the one by Frederick Ashton's for the Royal Danish Ballet and Rudolph Nureyev's for London Festival Ballet.

The two most widely performed productions are those by Kenneth MacMillan and John Cranko, both of whom were dancers with the Sadler's Wells Ballet before starting on their great careers as choreographers.

Kenneth MacMillan created his first professional ballet, *Danses Concertantes* in 1954. Just four years later he made his first ballet with Lyn Seymour, the start of a partnership which would include such ballets as *The Invitation* and *Anastasia*. In 1970 he succeeded Frederick Ashton as Director of the Royal Ballet and during that time created two more important full-length ballets *Manon* and *Mayerling*.

For some years John Cranko worked alongside Kenneth MacMillan producing ballets full of comic invention, such as *Pineapple Poll*. In 1961 he was invited to become Director of the Ballet in Stuttgart in Germany and it was there that he started his brilliant partnership with Marcia Haydée, just as MacMillan had with Lyn Seymour. As well as *Romeo and Juliet* he produced another Shakespeare ballet, the very funny *Taming of the Shrew*. By the time of his early death in 1973 he had created not only many superb ballets, but also a company of international importance. The ballet school in Stuttgart is now named in his memory and his ballerina, Marcia Haydée is director of his company.

Fonteyn and Nureyev during a televised performance of the balcony scene from *Romeo and Juliet*.

One of the cleverly arranged fight scenes from John Cranko's production for Stuttgart Ballet.

89

The Dance Notator

Most ballet companies now employ a dance notator; someone whose job it is to write down, *notate*, ballets as they are created. This 'score', rather like the one used for music, is used in rehearsals, to produce the ballet for other companies without having to rely on memory and to build up a library of definite information for the future.

Up to very recently, all ballets have been handed down from generation to generation by the dancers and ballet masters who made them. If a ballet was not performed for a long time and the dancers died, or even forgot it, the ballet was lost. We read of so many ballets by great choreographers of the past which were very successful, but we can only guess from old prints, photographs or drawings what they might have been like.

Nowadays we also use television video machines which can show instant replays during rehearsals just like those of football matches on your television. This is a perfect record of what happens, but it is not easy to learn from as you must try to think of everything the opposite way around, as if you were looking over your shoulder.

How magical this would have seemed to the very first people who tried to invent systems for writing down dances in the 15th and 16th centuries. Their attempts were really little more than their personal short-hand to remind them of their own ballets.

At the beginning of the 18th century Pierre Beauchamps, who was responsible for organizing the five positions, made a serious effort to have his system adopted widely, but it was not until the end of the 19th century that a system was devised which is important to us today.

Vladimir Stepanov was a dancer at the Imperial Ballet of the Tsar in St Petersburg. He used his system to write down many ballets by the great choreographer Marius Petipa, including *The Sleeping Beauty*.

His system was brought out of Russia and was used to produce the first classics for the Royal Ballet and a version of it is still taught to students of the Royal Ballet School.

In America today we find that the system called Labanotation is very widely used. It was invented in the 1920s and 1930s by Rudolph von Laban and was designed to suit all movement, not just dance.

In Britain and many other places the system known as Choreology is the most widespread. You may have seen the name 'Choreologist' in a programme at the ballet. Joan Benesh and Rudolph Benesh perfected their idea in the 1950s and it is the system used, for instance, to produce the ballets of Sir Frederick Ashton for the many companies around the world which perform them.

No system can truly convey the art of the ballet, but at least we can now be sure that the actual steps are reproduced accurately. The feeling, mood and characterisation that really make a performance will always have to be added by experienced dancers or the actual choreographer. The little touches of humour which make *La Fille Mal Gardée* such a charming ballet cannot be expressed on paper either in words or symbols.

Some ballets of simple steps, depending for their effect on truly great performances or on a particular style, may well still be lost for the future, but at least we now know that we are leaving behind a good record of all the great ballets being created today.

Left: The Ribbon Dance from *La Fille Mal Gardée*. Every step in the ballet has been written down in notation so that future generations of ballet enthusiasts can enjoy almost identical performances as we enjoy today.

Below: Benesch notation reads from left to right. The top line represents the top of the head, the second line is the top of the shoulders, the third line is the waist, the fourth line is the knees and the bottom line is the floor. By studying all the symbols, each one of which means something, dancers know exactly the positions they should adopt and steps they should make. Benesch notation made possible the science of choreology – the scientific study of movement. It was copyrighted in Britain in 1955 and among the companies who use it today are the Royal Ballet, Stuttgart Ballet, Scottish Ballet and Ballet Rambert. Both the Benesch and the Labanotation shown on this page were specially drawn for the book by the Royal Academy of Dancing which uses both systems and has a notation library.

Right: An example of Labanotation for the enchaînement of the Children's Syllabus of the Royal Academy of Dancing. The Labanotation is basically three vertical lines – the centre line dividing the right side of the body and the left side of the body. Each column represents a part of the body and when a movement symbol is placed in that column it will tell you what that part of the body is doing. The notation reads from bottom to top.

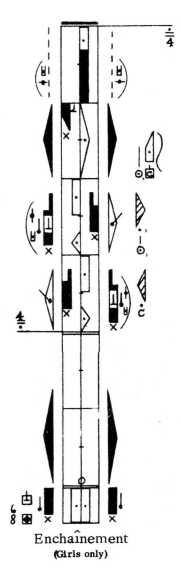

Enchaînement
(Girls only)

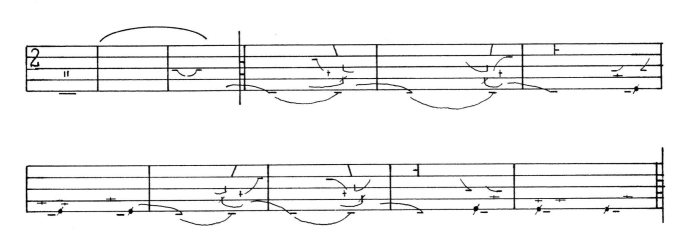

Mime

Right: The Ribbon Dance from *La Fille Mal Gardée*.

Mime was always used to tell the story in between the dance sequences of the earliest ballets. Gradually important choreographers such as Dauberval, who created the original *La Fille Mal Gardée* in 1789, began to break away from this tradition and found ways of carrying the story on through dances and natural, much less stylized, gestures.

The great choreographer Mikhail Fokine, too, believed that mime in the old-fashioned way held up the action and created works which were danced from beginning to end. Possibly you have seen his ballet *Les Sylphides* where the 'story' of the poet and the sylphs in the forest is shown entirely through dance. Of course even he did not do away with mime entirely. It is used

Love; as Albrecht tells of his devotion to Giselle or Prince Siegfried tells Odette, the Swan Queen.

Swear; as Albrecht confirms his love to Giselle or as Prince Siegfried does to Odile, the Black Swan, thinking she is his true love, Odette.

Marry; as Giselle in her madness remembers that she was betrothed to Albrecht or as the Princess Mother commands Prince Siegfried on his coming of age.

Hear or Listen; as Myrtha, the Queen of the Wilis hears someone approaching Giselle's grave or when Giselle's Mother calls the villagers to listen to the tale warning them about the Wilis.

in *Scheherazade*, the story taken from the Arabian Nights tales, when the great Shah is invited to go hunting or the Queen demands that the Golden Slave be let free. We also find it in *Giselle* or *Swan Lake*.

In the productions of these ballets which you see today much of the mime has been taken out. When these ballets were first produced, especially *Swan Lake* and *The Sleeping Beauty* they were much longer, partly on account of long mime passages which spelt out the story. These classic works are now so famous that choreographers making new versions of the ballets can afford to take it for granted that most of the audience know the story.

Important passages are, however, still used, some of great beauty. In *Swan Lake* for instance Odette the Swan Queen tells Prince Siegfried the story of how she was taken away by the evil magician von Rothbart. They are very moving even though parts are not very clear today. Have you noticed Odette explaining that the lake is made from her mother's tears?

In *Giselle* there are many examples of the good use of what we would call old-fashioned mime. Giselle's mother warns the villagers, and Giselle herself, of the Wilis who are in the forest. In the mad scene Giselle relives in mime little incidents which have happened earlier in the ballet; her dance with Albrecht, the plucking of the petals from the flower, to see if he truly loves her.

In a more recent work, Sir Frederick Ashton's *La Fille Mal Gardée*, there is a very simple and charming mime scene which uses few of the traditional gestures and relies instead on carefully selected natural movements which you will all recognize instantly.

Lise is in love with Colas, but her mother does not approve. After many attempts at keeping the two lovers apart Widow Simone locks Lise in the house, not realising that Colas has crept in when the harvesters come for their pay. Lise did not notice either and does not know that Colas is secretly spying on her. She daydreams about their wedding, fingering her long train. She imagines the children they will have, first one, then two, then three then four. She reads to them, she punishes them when they are naughty and she nurses the youngest . . . and then much to her embarrassment Colas jumps out.

This is a good example of the sort of mime we like today, but the traditional gestures will always be with us as part of the great classic tradition even though choreographers will find newer and better ways of telling their stories through pure dance.

Here are some examples of mime gestures which you will come across most often when you see the great classic ballets. As G. B. L. Wilson explains in his *Dictionary of Ballet*, to put into words a series of mime gestures you should follow French rather than English. For example you would say 'I you love' for 'I love you'.

Call; Myrtha summons the Wilis from the depths of the forest to welcome Giselle to their ranks.

Ask; As Giselle pleads to Myrtha for Albrecht's life.

No or Not; as Myrtha refuses Giselle's plea.

Dance; as Albrecht must do until he dies as Myrtha's command, or more happily in many joyous *pas de deux* such as *Flower Festival*.

Lynn Seymour, one of the greatest dramatic dancers of our time, created many roles for Kenneth Macmillan including the part of *Anastasia* which she is dancing here.

Index

The publishers would like to thank the following organisations and individuals for their kind permission to reproduce the photographs in this book: –

All special photography by Jesse Davis; Zoe Dominic: 2, 6, 7, 8, 82, 83, 87, 88, 89; Fred Fehl: Endpapers, 34, 47, 71; Gil Montalverne: 70; Pictor: 30–31; London Festival Ballet (Anthony Crickmay): Contents (4), 14–15, 24, 73; Leslie E. Spatt: 95; The Wallace Collection (J. R. Freeman): 70. All other photographs by Mike Davis Studio.

First published by
Octopus Books Limited
59 Grosvenor Street
London W1

© Octopus Books Limited 1979

ISBN 0 7064 1021 1

Printed in Italy
nuova grafica moderna s.p.a. - verona